YOUR recipe could appear in our next cookbook!

Share your tried & true family favorites with us instantly at
www.gooseberrypatch.com
If you'd rather jot 'em down by hand, just mail this form to...
Gooseberry Patch • Cookbooks – Call for Recipes
2500 Farmers Dr., #110 • Columbus, OH 43235

If your recipe is selected for a book, you'll receive a FREE copy!

Please share only your original recipes or those that you have made your own over the years.

Recipe Name:

Number of Servings:

Any fond memories about this recipe? Special touches you like to add
or handy shortcuts?

Ingredients (include specific measurements):

D1608774

Instructions (continue on back if needed):

Special Code: **cookbookspage**

Over ➤

Extra space for recipe if needed:

Tell us about yourself...

Your complete contact information is needed so that we can send you your FREE cookbook, if your recipe is published. Phone numbers and email addresses are kept private and will only be used if we have questions about your recipe.

Name:

Address:

City: State: Zip:

Email:

Daytime Phone:

Thank you! Vickie & Jo Ann

Gooseberry Patch
2500 Farmers Dr., #110
Columbus, OH 43235

www.gooseberrypatch.com

1·800·854·6673

Copyright 2012, Gooseberry Patch 978-1-61281-054-6
First Printing, March, 2012

Do you have a tried & true recipe...

tip, craft or memory that you'd like to see featured in a **Gooseberry
Patch** cookbook? Visit our website at **www.gooseberrypatch.com**
to share them with us instantly. If you'd rather jot them down by hand,
use the handy form in the front of this book and send them to...

Gooseberry Patch
Attn: Cookbook Dept.
2500 Farmers Dr., #110
Columbus, OH 43235

Don't forget to include the number of servings your recipe makes,
plus your name, address, phone number and email address.
If we select your recipe, your name will appear right along
with it...and you'll receive a **FREE** copy of the cookbook!

Contents

Dedication

Dedicated to all our friends who love to
gather family & friends 'round the table...
Christmastime and any time!

Appreciation

A big merry thank-you for sharing
your family's favorite dishes and
jolly holiday memories.

Cozy Christmas Brunch

Orange Spiced French Toast

Katie Majeske
Denver, PA

This recipe comes from one of our favorite B&Bs...it's so delicious!

1 loaf French bread, sliced
4 eggs
2/3 c. orange juice
1/3 c. milk
1/4 c. sugar

1 t. vanilla extract
1/4 t. cinnamon
1/8 t. nutmeg
1/4 c. butter, melted

Arrange bread slices in a single layer in an ungreased 13"x9" baking pan. In a bowl with an electric mixer on low speed, beat remaining ingredients except butter. Pour egg mixture over bread, turning slices over to coat both sides. Cover and refrigerate for 2 to 24 hours. Spread butter in a 15"x10" jelly-roll pan. Arrange bread slices in a single layer on top of butter. Bake, uncovered, at 400 degrees for 20 to 25 minutes, until lightly golden, turning slices once halfway through baking time. Serve immediately with warm Orange Syrup. Serves 6 to 8.

Orange Syrup:

1/2 c. butter
1/2 c. sugar
1/3 c. frozen orange juice
    concentrate

1/2 c. chopped pecans

In a saucepan over low heat, combine butter, sugar and orange juice concentrate. Stir until butter is melted; do not boil. Cool for 10 minutes; beat with an electric mixer on low speed until thickened. Stir in pecans.

Little extras for Christmas morning...a small wrapped gift at each place setting, soft holiday music in the background and no lights allowed except those on the tree. So magical!

Cozy Christmas
❧ Brunch ☙

Baked Hard-Boiled Egg Casserole

Leah Beyer
Flat Rock, IN

Whenever we get together with my family, this brunch casserole is a must!

1/2 c. butter
1/2 c. all-purpose flour
1/2 t. salt
1/4 t. white pepper
4 c. milk

1 doz. eggs, hard-boiled, peeled
   and sliced
1 lb. bacon, crisply cooked and
   crumbled
2 c. shredded Cheddar cheese

In a saucepan over medium heat, melt butter. Add flour, salt and pepper; whisk until smooth. Gradually whisk in milk. Bring mixture to a boil; cook and stir for 2 minutes, or until thickened. In a 3-quart casserole dish, spread 1/3 of butter mixture, followed by 1/3 each of eggs, bacon and cheese. Repeat layers twice, ending with cheese. Bake, covered, at 350 degrees for 30 minutes, or until hot and bubbly. Casserole may be refrigerated overnight before baking; add 10 minutes to baking time. Serves 6 to 8.

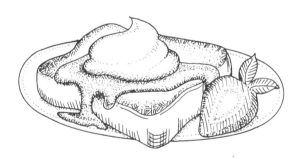

Whip up a luscious topping to dollop on pancakes, French toast and slices of fruit bread...yum! Combine 3/4 cup whipping cream, 2 tablespoons softened cream cheese and one tablespoon powdered sugar. Beat with an electric mixer on medium speed until soft peaks form. Keep refrigerated in a small covered crock.

Quiche Muffins

Elizabeth Cisneros
Eastvale, CA

Wonderful for an easy Christmas morning breakfast. You can prepare the muffins in advance, refrigerate overnight and pop them in the oven while you are checking out the Christmas stockings.

1/2 c. fresh spinach, chopped
3 T. onion, minced
1 t. olive oil
1/4 c. butter, melted
1 c. sour cream
1/2 c. milk
4 eggs, beaten
1/2 t. garlic powder
1/4 t. pepper
1/2 c. grated Parmesan cheese
1-1/2 c. biscuit baking mix
1 c. shredded sharp Cheddar cheese, divided
1 c. bacon or ham, cooked and chopped

Spray 18 muffin cups with non-stick vegetable spray or line with paper baking cups; set aside. In a microwave-safe bowl, combine spinach, onion and oil; microwave on high setting for 45 seconds, or until spinach is wilted. In a large bowl, whisk together butter, sour cream, milk, eggs, garlic powder, pepper and Parmesan cheese. Stir in baking mix; whisk until smooth. Add spinach mixture, 1/2 cup Cheddar cheese and bacon or ham; stir until well combined. Spoon mixture into muffin cups, filling 2/3 full. Sprinkle tops with remaining Cheddar cheese. Bake at 350 degrees for 30 to 35 minutes, until tops are golden and a toothpick inserted in the centers tests clean. Serve warm. Makes 18.

A neat trick when baking muffins! Grease muffin cups on the bottoms and just halfway up the sides... muffins will bake up nicely domed on top.

Cozy Christmas Brunch

Christmas Morning Eggs

Joyce Maltby
Cheboygan, MI

I've made this overnight egg bake every Christmas since my four children were little. My kids still call this dish "Christmas Eggs" even though they're all grown up now.

1 lb. ground pork sausage or
    ham, cooked and chopped
2 slices day-old bread, cubed
6 eggs, beaten
2 c. milk

2 c. shredded favorite-flavor
    cheese
1 t. dry mustard
1 t. salt
1/2 t. pepper

Combine all ingredients, mixing well. Pour into an ungreased 13"x9" baking pan. Cover and refrigerate overnight. Bake, uncovered, at 350 degrees for 45 minutes, or until eggs are set. Serves 8.

On Christmas morning every year, my brother and I would run into our parents' room to wake them. Our parents would groggily go downstairs to see if Santa had come during the night, leaving my brother and me cozy in their bed, surrounded by the warmth of their electric blanket. A few minutes after they'd gone downstairs, the song "A Christmas Festival" would start playing and we knew that was our cue to go to see what Santa had brought us! I have continued the tradition of playing this song every Christmas morning for my kids, too.

–Christy Jones, Barrington, NH

24-Hour Never-Fail Cheese Soufflé

Marybeth Summers
Medford, OR

Mmm...so tasty for brunch!

12 to 14 thick slices white
    bread, crusts trimmed
4 eggs, beaten
2-1/2 c. milk
1/2 t. dry mustard
1/3 c. green pepper, chopped

1/2 c. sweet onion, sliced
16-oz. pkg. shredded sharp
    Cheddar cheese
1 c. cooked ham, diced
Optional: paprika

Cut bread slices into cubes. In a large bowl, combine bread and remaining ingredients except paprika; mix well. Pour into a greased 3-quart casserole dish. Cover and refrigerate overnight. Bake, uncovered, at 350 degrees for one hour, or until golden. Before serving, sprinkle with paprika, if desired. Serves 6 to 8.

My all-time favorite childhood memory is of the special Christmas countdown rings that my neighbor, affectionately known as Aunt Opie, would make for me. She would take pretty old Christmas cards and make a chain of 24 rings for me to tear off each day between December 1 and Christmas Eve. At the top, there would be a beautiful handmade ornament for my tree. I carry on this tradition with my three children and niece as a way of honoring and remembering such a wonderful woman!

–Lisa Ellsworth, Sparta, MO

Cozy Christmas
Brunch

Sugarplum Bacon

Brenda Hager
Nancy, KY

*I love this crunchy, sweet combination! It's wonderful
served for breakfast or as an appetizer.*

1/2 lb. sliced bacon, room
    temperature

1/2 c. brown sugar, packed
1 t. cinnamon

Cut each slice of bacon in half crosswise. Combine brown sugar and
cinnamon in a shallow bowl. Dredge each piece of bacon in brown
sugar mixture; twist and place in an ungreased 13"x9" baking pan.
Bake, uncovered, at 350 degrees for 15 to 20 minutes, until bacon is
crisp and sugar is bubbly. Remove slices to aluminum foil to cool.
Serve at room temperature. Makes 18 to 24 pieces.

Holiday Sausage Ring

Gen Cornish
Arizona City, AZ

*We traditionally host Christmas brunch at our house. Everyone
always expects to see this sausage ring on the table loaded with fluffy
scrambled eggs in the center. It's definitely a family favorite!*

2 lbs. ground pork sausage
2 eggs, beaten
2 T. onion, grated

1-1/2 c. dry bread crumbs
1/4 c. fresh parsley, chopped

Lightly grease a 9" ring mold. In a large bowl, combine all ingredients;
mix well. Pack into mold. Bake, uncovered, at 350 degrees for
20 minutes. Remove from oven; drain. Return to oven; bake
20 minutes longer. Turn out onto a warm platter. Serves 8 to 10.

Don't wait until Christmas Day
to use your festive holiday dishes...
use them all season long for
a daily dose of cheer!

Strawberry & Raspberry Strata

Sonya Labbe
West Hollywood, CA

*Bursting with berries, this is a dish that always makes it
onto our Sunday brunch table. You can make it
all year 'round with frozen berries.*

4 eggs, beaten
1/2 c. low-fat ricotta cheese
3 T. sugar
1 c. milk
1/4 c. orange juice
1/2 c. honey

4 slices bread, torn into
   1-inch pieces
1/2 c. frozen raspberries, thawed
   and drained
1/2 c. frozen strawberries,
   thawed and drained

In a large bowl, combine eggs, ricotta cheese and sugar. Stir in milk,
orange juice, honey and bread. Stir to combine. Gently fold in berries.
Transfer to a lightly greased 2-quart casserole dish. Cover with plastic
wrap; refrigerate at least 2 hours to overnight. Remove plastic wrap;
bake, covered, at 350 degrees for 40 minutes, or until golden on top
and cooked through. Let stand 5 minutes before serving. Spoon into
dishes to serve. Serves 4.

At Christmas play and make good cheer,
For Christmas comes but once a year.

–Thomas Tusser

Cozy Christmas
Brunch

Apple-Cinnamon Puff

Paulette Alexander
Newfoundland, Canada

*This is one of my favorite brunch recipes. It's not too sweet...
somewhat of a cross between a pancake, soufflé and quiche!
Everybody who tries it simply loves it.*

1/3 c. butter, melted and divided
3 eggs, beaten
3/4 c. all-purpose flour
3/4 c. milk
1 T. sugar

1/8 t. salt
3 apples, peeled, cored and
  sliced
1/4 c. brown sugar, packed
1 t. cinnamon

Place 2 tablespoons melted butter in a medium bowl. Add eggs, flour,
milk, sugar and salt; beat with an electric mixer on medium speed until
smooth. Set aside. To a cast-iron or ovenproof skillet over medium
heat, add remaining butter; add apples, brown sugar and cinnamon.
Cook, stirring occasionally, until apples are golden, about 10 to
15 minutes. Remove from heat; pour batter over apples in skillet.
Bake, uncovered, at 350 degrees for 15 to 20 minutes, until puffed
and golden. If desired, invert onto serving plate, scraping any
remaining apples and syrup from pan and spooning over top. Serve
warm. Serves 4 to 6.

Snap a photo of your family
in the same place and same
position each year...it will
be a sweet reminder of
how the kids have grown!

13

Apple Cider Breakfast Oats

Kristy Wells
Candler, FL

I came up with this simple recipe while pregnant with my youngest daughter. It has a natural sweetness without any added sugar, making it taste so good that it should be bad for you, but it's not!

2 c. apple cider or juice
2/3 c. golden raisins
2/3 c. chopped pecans
1 t. apple pie spice

2 T. butter
2 T. maple syrup
1 c. steel-cut oats, uncooked
1/4 c. fat-free half-and-half

In a saucepan, combine all ingredients except oats and half-and-half. Bring to a boil; stir in oats and continue to boil until mixture thickens and oats are fully cooked, about 15 minutes. Remove from heat; stir in half-and-half. Serve immediately. Make 2 servings.

Get a head start on holiday festivities! Soon after the leaves begin to fall, check your local newspaper or city's website for once-a-year events like craft bazaars, storytelling, caroling and the lighting of the Christmas tree in Town Square.

Whole-Wheat Gingerbread Pancakes

Lisa McClelland
Columbus, OH

This is one of the first recipes I created when I was a teenager. It quickly became a staple for our holiday breakfasts. For a really yummy touch, skip the maple syrup...spread each pancake with some butter and lemon curd, roll up and eat!

1 c. whole-wheat flour	1/4 t. nutmeg
1 c. all-purpose flour	1/8 t. cardamom
1 T. baking powder	2-1/4 c. plain yogurt
1/2 t. salt	1/4 c. molasses
1 T. ground ginger	2 T. butter, melted
1-1/2 t. cinnamon	2 eggs, beaten
1/2 t. allspice	Optional: 1 to 2 T. milk
1/4 t. ground cloves	

In a large bowl, combine flours, baking powder, salt and spices. In a separate bowl, whisk together yogurt and molasses. Add butter and eggs; mix well. Add yogurt mixture to flour mixture; stir well. If the mixture is too thick, add milk to reach desired consistency. Pour batter by 1/4 cupfuls onto a hot, lightly greased griddle. Cook until batter starts to bubble, about 3 minutes. Flip pancakes; cook an additional 2 to 3 minutes, until golden. Serves 4.

Festoon a doorway or mantel with a garland of gingerbread people. After cutting out cookie dough, make a small hole in each "hand" with a drinking straw. Bake and decorate cookies, then tie them together side-by-side with narrow ribbon threaded through the holes.

Jenn's Crème Brûlée French Toast

Jennifer Donnelly
Woodlawn, TN

*I discovered a similar recipe in a cookbook and have since
reworked it to satisfy my family's tastes. They love it!*

1/2 c. butter
1 c. brown sugar, packed
2 T. corn syrup
1 c. chopped walnuts
12 slices Texas toast bread
5 eggs, beaten

1-1/2 c. half-and-half
1 t. vanilla extract
1 t. cinnamon
1/4 t. salt
Optional: additional cinnamon,
    maple syrup

In a small saucepan over medium heat, combine butter, brown sugar
and corn syrup; cook and stir until smooth. Pour mixture into an
17"x12" greased jelly-roll pan. Spread to cover surface; sprinkle
walnuts evenly over butter mixture. Arrange bread in a single layer to
cover nuts and butter mixture. In a bowl, combine eggs, half-and-half,
vanilla, cinnamon and salt. Using a ladle, spoon egg mixture over each
bread slice. Sprinkle with more cinnamon, if desired. Cover and
refrigerate overnight. Bake, uncovered, at 350 degrees for 30 minutes.
Serve warm with syrup, if using. If not serving immediately, turn each
slice of bread over once to prevent bread from sticking to the pan.
Serves 6 to 8.

Honey-Pecan Syrup

Kathy Grashoff
Fort Wayne, IN

Buttery, sweet pecans...yum!

1/2 c. pecan halves, toasted
3/4 c. honey

1/4 c. butter

Combine all ingredients in a saucepan; cook over low heat, stirring
occasionally, until butter is melted and mixture is hot. Serve warm
over waffles or pancakes. Makes about 1-1/2 cups.

Cozy Christmas
Brunch

Sour Cream Coffee Cake

Emily Salsky
Tempe, AZ

My mother makes this coffee cake every Christmas morning. When my siblings and I were younger, it would always be baking when we came downstairs to open presents. Now that we're older, she still makes it but not as early! The scent of this cake will always bring back fond memories. I look forward to making it for my own children someday.

1-3/4 c. all-purpose flour
1 t. baking powder
1 t. baking soda
1 c. sugar
1/4 t. salt
1-1/2 c. butter, softened

2 eggs, beaten
1 c. sour cream
3/4 c. brown sugar, packed
1 T. cinnamon
3/4 c. chopped nuts

In a bowl, combine flour, baking powder, baking soda, sugar, salt, butter, eggs and sour cream. In a separate bowl, combine brown sugar, cinnamon and nuts. Pour half the batter into a greased tube or Bundt® pan; sprinkle with half the brown sugar mixture. Repeat layers once. Bake at 350 degrees for 35 to 45 minutes, until cake tests clean with a skewer. Serves 12.

An extra-special touch for your holiday brunch...festive shaped sugar cubes! In a bowl, combine 1/2 cup white or brown sugar with just enough water to make a paste-like consistency. Press firmly into a candy mold, filling cups about halfway. Let dry overnight, then carefully remove cubes.

Jingle Bell Java

Teresa Firth
Knoxville, TN

We enjoy this coffee drink from Thanksgiving to New Year's Day. For added flavor and fun, we toss in marshmallows and stir with a candy cane. This mix also looks nice layered in a jar...a perfect gift!

2 c. powdered non-dairy creamer
1-1/2 c. baking cocoa
1-1/2 c. instant coffee granules
1-1/2 c. sugar
1 t. cinnamon
1/2 t. nutmeg

In a bowl, combine all ingredients, mixing well. Store in an airtight container. To serve, add 3 tablespoons to a mug and add boiling water to fill. Makes about 30 servings.

Snowflake Hot Cocoa

Gina Forman
Peru, IN

We always make a big batch of this rich cocoa at the office right before Christmas break. It really gets us in the mood for the holidays and it stays nice and warm in the slow cooker.

2 c. whipping cream
6 c. milk
1 t. vanilla extract
11-oz. pkg. white chocolate
  chips

Garnish: whipped cream, chocolate syrup, candy canes, crushed crème de menthe thins

In a slow cooker, combine all ingredients except garnish. Cover and cook on low setting for 2 to 2-1/2 hours, stirring occasionally, until chocolate chips are melted. Stir before serving; garnish as desired. Makes 12 servings.

Make color copies of vintage Christmas postcards...they make such pretty nostalgic gift tags and jar labels.

Cozy Christmas Brunch

Chicken & Asparagus Quiche
Melissa Knight
Athens, AL

My mother's wonderful quiche recipe is perfect for Christmas brunch!

2 9-inch pie crusts
2 T. butter
2 T. olive oil
1 T. garlic, minced
1 onion, chopped
1 bunch asparagus, trimmed and
    cut into 1-inch pieces
2 boneless, skinless chicken
    breasts, diced

3 eggs, beaten
1 c. half-and-half
1 t. dry mustard
salt and pepper to taste
2 c. shredded Monterey Jack
    cheese, divided

Place pie crusts in two 9" pie plates; bake at 450 degrees for 10 to 12 minutes, until lightly golden. Meanwhile, in a large skillet, melt butter and olive oil over medium heat. Sauté garlic, onion and asparagus for 5 to 7 minutes, until asparagus is crisp-tender. With a slotted spoon, remove vegetables from skillet, leaving as much of the butter mixture as possible. Add chicken to skillet; sauté for 7 to 8 minutes, until fully cooked. Remove skillet from heat. In a bowl, whisk together remaining ingredients except cheeses. Sprinkle 1/2 cup cheese in each pie crust. Layer half the chicken in each crust, followed by half the veggies and half the egg mixture. Top with remaining cheese. Bake, uncovered, at 375 degrees for 30 to 35 minutes. Makes 2 quiches; each serves 4 to 6.

Use an old galvanized wash tub as a farmhouse-inspired disguise for your tree stand.

Gwam's Poached Pears

Sandy Perry
Bakersfield, CA

I love pears, and these make breakfast time extra special.

6 pears
2 4-inch cinnamon sticks
4 c. apple cider

1-1/2 c. vanilla yogurt
cinnamon to taste
Garnish: nutmeg

Place whole unpeeled pears in a large saucepan; add cinnamon sticks and pour apple cider over top. Bring to a boil; simmer, uncovered, about 25 minutes, or until pears are soft and can be easily pierced with a knife. Reserve 1/4 cup cider; discard remaining cider and cinnamon sticks, or save for another use. In a bowl, combine yogurt, cinnamon and reserved cider. To serve, place a pear on a dessert plate and spoon some yogurt mixture over top; sprinkle with nutmeg. Makes 6.

Spiced Pineapple Bananas

Jim Bohner
Harrisburg, PA

Tired of banana bread? This is a great recipe for using up your overripe bananas. Try other fruit combinations by using your favorite-flavor jelly or preserves in place of the pineapple.

3 bananas
2 T. butter, softened and divided
1/3 c. brown sugar, packed
2 T. canned crushed pineapple,
   drained

2 T. pineapple juice
1 t. cinnamon
Garnish: chopped nuts

Cut bananas in half crosswise, then cut each piece lengthwise. Using one tablespoon butter, grease the bottom of an 8"x8" baking pan. Arrange bananas in a single layer in pan; set aside. Combine remaining butter, pineapple, juice and cinnamon in a saucepan over medium-high heat; bring to a boil and cook for 2 minutes, stirring constantly. Pour mixture over bananas. Broil under low heat for 3 minutes, or until hot and bubbly and bananas are tender. Garnish with nuts. Serves 4 to 6.

Cozy Christmas
Brunch

Crab Quiche

Pamela Ballance
British Columbia, Canada

Whenever I make this quiche, people think I can really cook...but they don't realize how easy it is to make! This quiche also freezes well, so it's a perfect dish for the busy holiday season.

5 T. all-purpose flour
1/2 c. mayonnaise
2 eggs, beaten
1/2 c. milk
1/2 c. green onions, chopped

8-oz. pkg. shredded Swiss cheese
6-oz. can crabmeat, drained and flaked
9-inch pie crust

In a large bowl, combine flour, mayonnaise, eggs and milk. Stir in onions, cheese and crabmeat. Pour into unbaked pie crust. Bake, uncovered, at 350 degrees for 40 to 45 minutes. Serves 4 to 6.

At Christmas, my mother always gave us kids new pajamas to wear on Christmas Eve. It was so exciting to see what new gown or PJs I would have for the big night. My parents did not have much money, but they always managed to have those new pajamas for us. Now, as a parent, I do the same with my little boy, Michael, with one little difference...the Peek Elves deliver them to our house. The week before Christmas, our doorbell rings and a bag is found on the stoop. Michael is so excited to see what is inside the bag. If it is snowing out, he looks for the footprints left by the Elves. If a really big snowstorm hits, the Elves have been known to bring bonus gifts, such as snowmen kits to play with outside. I hope my son carries on this tradition with his children someday. To watch him makes a lifetime's worth of memories.

–Susie Cliffel, Wadsworth, OH

Country Biscuits & Gravy

Kathy Smith
Cincinnati, OH

*My husband spent a lot of time with his grandma in Kentucky
and he learned to make this gravy from her. It's very easy to
make and tastes so yummy on a chilly winter morning.*

1 lb. ground pork sausage
5 to 6 T. all-purpose flour
3 c. milk

salt and pepper to taste
6 to 8 biscuits, split

In a skillet over medium-high heat, cook and crumble sausage until
well browned; do not drain. Reduce heat to medium-low; sprinkle
flour over sausage. Add milk; cook, stirring constantly, until mixture
thickens. Add salt and pepper. Serve gravy ladled over biscuits.
Serves 4 to 6.

A no-mess method for greasing and flouring baking pans:
Simply grease pan, sprinkle generously with flour,
cover with plastic wrap and shake!

Cozy Christmas
Brunch

Jane's Fiesta Eggs

Diana Krol
Nickerson, KS

*My friend Jane served this dish at our Bible study brunch. It is
the best egg casserole I've ever eaten!*

10 eggs, beaten
2 c. shredded Monterey Jack
cheese
2 c. shredded Cheddar cheese
2 c. cottage cheese
2 4-oz. cans chopped green
chiles

1/2 c. butter, melted
1/2 c. all-purpose flour
1 t. baking powder
1/2 t. salt
Garnish: salsa

In a large bowl, combine all ingredients except salsa; mix well. Pour
into a buttered 13"x 9" baking pan. Bake, uncovered, at 350 degrees
for 45 to 50 minutes, until edges are golden and center is set. Serve
with salsa. Serves 8 to 10.

Nicki's Breakfast Frittata

Nicki Hill
Louisville, KY

*I love to mix up this frittata in my favorite cast-iron
skillet...my ladies' prayer group loves it!*

6 eggs, beaten
2 T. milk
1 c. shredded Cheddar cheese
1 t. dried parsley

2 green onions, chopped
1/2 c. cooked ham, diced
1/2 t. salt
1/4 t. pepper

In a large bowl, combine all ingredients; mix well. Heat a greased
cast-iron or ovenproof skillet over medium heat; pour egg mixture into
skillet. Cook over low heat, without stirring, until egg mixture is almost
cooked through, about 4 minutes. Transfer to oven and bake,
uncovered, at 350 degrees for about 8 minutes longer, until cheese
is melted and eggs are set. Slice into wedges to serve. Serves 6.

Sausage Strata

Shannon Reents
Loudonville, OH

The ladies at my church would put breakfast together once in awhile for churchgoers. This is a recipe I made often. You can substitute chopped ham or bacon for the sausage, if you'd like.

2 T. butter, softened
16 slices white bread, crusts
  trimmed
1-1/2 lbs. ground pork sausage,
  browned and drained
8 slices sharp Cheddar cheese

10 eggs, beaten
3 c. milk
1/2 t. dry mustard
1/2 t. salt
3/4 c. cornflake cereal, crushed
1/4 c. butter, melted

Spread butter over 8 bread slices on one side. Place slices, butter-side down, in a 13"x9" glass baking pan. Layer with sausage, cheese and remaining bread. In a bowl, combine eggs, milk, mustard and salt. Pour over bread. Cover and refrigerate for 8 hours to overnight. Remove from refrigerator 1-1/2 hours before baking. Toss cereal with butter; sprinkle over top. Bake, uncovered, at 350 degrees for one hour and 20 minutes. Let stand 10 minutes; cut into squares to serve. Serves 10 to 12.

Mix up some figgy butter! In a bowl, combine one cup softened butter with a 10-ounce jar fig preserves, 1/2 teaspoon vanilla extract and 1/8 teaspoon nutmeg. Mix well. Transfer to a sheet of parchment paper, roll into a log and chill for at least one hour. To serve, simply slice what you need.

Cozy Christmas
Brunch

Kitchen Cupboard Waffles

James Bohner
Harrisburg, PA

Every year we schedule one day for our family to go out Christmas shopping. Before we leave, we have a special tradition...warm waffles and maple syrup for breakfast. All the ingredients for this quick & easy recipe can be found in your kitchen cupboard!

2 c. all-purpose flour
4 t. baking powder
2 T. sugar
1 t. salt

2 eggs, separated
1-1/2 c. milk
6 T. butter, melted

In a bowl, combine flour, baking powder, sugar and salt. In a small bowl, beat egg yolks and milk; add to flour mixture. Stir in butter. Beat egg whites until stiff; fold into flour mixture. Cook in a greased waffle iron according to manufacturer's instructions. Serve topped with Buttery Maple Syrup. Serves 6.

Buttery Maple Syrup:

1/2 c. maple syrup
1/2 c. water
1/4 c. butter

Optional: cinnamon, fresh chopped fruit, jam or preserves

Combine all ingredients in a saucepan. Cook and stir over medium heat until butter is melted. If desired, stir in optional ingredients; warm through. Makes about 1-1/4 cups.

Provide a warm glow for holiday gatherings. Set out fragrant candles in old-fashioned canning jars tied with holiday ribbons.

Grandma Cook's Applesauce Cake

Judy Weyer
Cincinnati, OH

My mother made this delicious cake every Christmas for family & friends. Although she always called it Applesauce Cake, it is actually more bread-like than cake-like. Now, I make cakes for my daughters every Christmas. We like to eat our slices slathered with creamy butter!

2 c. sugar
1/2 c. butter, softened
5 eggs, beaten
1 c. applesauce
3 c. all-purpose flour
1 t. baking soda

1/4 t. salt
1 t. cinnamon
1/2 t. ground cloves
1 c. chopped walnuts
1 c. raisins

In a large bowl, combine sugar, butter, eggs and applesauce. In a separate bowl, mix flour, baking soda, salt, cinnamon and cloves. Add flour mixture to sugar mixture; mix well. Fold in walnuts and raisins. Pour into a greased Bundt® pan. Bake at 350 degrees for one hour, or until a toothpick inserted into cake tests clean. Makes 18 to 24 servings.

Create a new cake stand for your Christmas brunch...just place a plate on top of a short wide-mouth vase for a striking display. If a permanent adhesive is desired, use china glue; if not, simply lift the plate from the vase before cutting and serving the cake.

Cozy Christmas
Brunch

The Best Scones Ever

Kathryn Southwick-Hess
Walla Walla, WA

This is a favorite "go-to" scone recipe because it is can be dressed up in so many ways. Be sure to let the dough rest for 10 minutes before baking. This ensures tall, happy scones.

3 c. all-purpose flour
1/3 c. plus 2 T. sugar, divided
2-1/2 t. baking powder
1/2 t. baking soda
1/2 t. salt
3/4 c. butter, softened and sliced
1 c. buttermilk

Optional: 1 c. cinnamon chips,
   white chocolate chips,
   raisins or currants, or
   1/2 c. crystallized ginger,
   dried apricots or dried
   cherries, chopped

In a large bowl, stir together flour, 1/3 cup sugar, baking powder, baking soda and salt. Using a pastry blender, cut butter into flour mixture until mixture is coarse and crumbly. Add buttermilk; stir with a fork until a soft dough forms. Add optional ingredients, if using. Gather dough into a ball, pressing gently to hold together. Turn out onto a lightly floured surface; knead about a dozen times, or until dough is no longer sticky. Cut dough ball in half. Roll or pat dough into a 1/2-inch thick, 7-inch circle. Sprinkle with remaining sugar. Cut circle into 6 to 8 wedges; place on ungreased baking sheets. Repeat steps with remaining dough. Allow dough to rest 10 minutes. Bake at 425 degrees for 10 to 12 minutes, until golden. Cool on wire racks. Makes 12 to 16.

Most quick bread, scone and biscuit recipes don't call for more than one cup of buttermilk. If you don't want to buy a whole quart, you can replace it with soured milk. To make your own at home, add one tablespoon of white vinegar or lemon juice to one cup of whole milk, and let stand for five minutes.

Loaded Breakfast Loaf

Jeannette Groves
Ooltewah, TN

My husband and I love to cook together! We're always creating new dishes. This one's a keeper.

8 eggs, beaten
3 c. self-rising flour
1 T. powdered sugar
1 T. baking powder
3/4 c. shortening

1-3/4 c. buttermilk
1 thick slice cooked ham, diced
4 slices cheese
1 egg, beaten

In a greased skillet over medium heat, stir eggs and cook until scrambled; set aside. In a bowl, combine flour, sugar, baking powder, shortening and buttermilk. On parchment paper, knead dough about a dozen times, or until no longer sticky; roll out to a 12-inch square, trimming edges if needed. Spread scrambled eggs, ham and cheese evenly over dough; roll up jelly-roll style. Fold in ends; lift parchment paper and transfer to a lightly greased 13"x9" baking pan. Brush loaf with beaten egg. Bake, uncovered, at 375 degrees for 20 to 25 minutes, until golden. Slice to serve. Serves 6 to 8.

Try this shortcut for making Loaded Breakfast Loaf...just start with a thawed one-pound loaf of frozen bread dough!

Cozy Christmas
Brunch

Overnight Shrimp Grits & Eggs

Dorothy Benson
Baton Rouge, LA

This dish takes awhile to make, but it's well worth the effort!

5 c. water	1 T. butter
1/2 t. salt	1 T. oil
1 c. quick-cooking grits, uncooked	1 lb. asparagus, trimmed
1/2 t. pepper	8 eggs
3/4 c. grated Parmesan cheese	Garnish: grated Parmesan cheese
1/3 c. all-purpose flour	

In a large saucepan over high heat, bring water and salt to a boil; slowly stir in grits. Cook for 8 minutes or until thickened; whisk in pepper and cheese. Press grits mixture into a lightly greased 11"x7" baking pan. Cover and refrigerate 8 hours to overnight. Cut grits into 3-inch squares; lightly dredge in flour. In a skillet over medium heat, melt butter and oil; fry grits squares for 3 to 4 minutes on each side, until golden. Steam asparagus until crisp-tender, about 5 minutes. In a pan of simmering water, poach eggs. Top each grits square with one to 2 asparagus spears and a poached egg. Cover with Creamy Shrimp Sauce. Serve warm. Garnish with cheese. Makes 8 servings.

Creamy Shrimp Sauce:

2-1/2 T. butter, divided	1 shallot, sliced
1 lb. medium shrimp, cleaned	1-1/2 T. all-purpose flour
14-oz. can chicken broth	1 c. whipping cream

In a skillet over medium heat, melt one tablespoon butter. Add shrimp; cook and stir for 5 minutes, until shrimp turn pink. Chop shrimp; set aside. Add chicken broth and shallot; bring to a boil. Remove from heat. Meanwhile, melt remaining butter in a saucepan over medium heat. Whisk in flour; cook, stirring constantly, for one minute. Slowly whisk in broth mixture; cook until slightly thickened, about one minute. Stir in cream; reduce heat. Add shrimp; heat through.

Monkey Bread Muffins

Vickie

A mini version of a holiday favorite!

12 frozen dinner rolls, thawed
   but still chilled
6 T. butter, melted

2 T. corn syrup
1/2 c. brown sugar, packed
2 t. cinnamon

Cut each dinner roll into 6 pieces. In a bowl, combine butter and corn syrup; stir until well mixed. In a separate bowl, combine sugar and cinnamon. Dip each roll piece in butter mixture and then in cinnamon-sugar. Place 6 pieces in each greased cup of a 12-cup muffin tin. Cover with plastic wrap that has been sprayed with non-stick vegetable spray; let dough rise until double in size. Remove wrap; bake at 350 degrees for 15 to 20 minutes. Cool in pan for 3 to 4 minutes. Makes one dozen.

Maple Icing

Kristie Rigo
Friedens, PA

This creamy icing is good on anything, but it really shines on cinnamon rolls!

1/4 c. butter, softened
1/3 c. evaporated milk
1-1/2 t. maple flavoring

1/8 t. salt
2-1/2 to 3-1/2 c. powdered
   sugar

With an electric mixer on medium speed, beat butter until fluffy. Add milk, maple flavoring and salt; mix well. Add powdered sugar 1/2 cup at a time until icing reaches desired consistency. Makes enough to frost one pan of cinnamon rolls.

Why not host a weekend brunch for family & friends? It's a great break from all the evening parties this time of year.

Christmas
Brunch Menu
Company's Coming
Breakfast Casserole
Aunt June's
Yummy Potatoes
Grandma's Sweet Rolls
Coffee & Juice

Cozy Christmas
Brunch

Orange Rolls

Tammie Douglas
Ossian, IN

This is a fun twist on the traditional cinnamon roll. We love them any time of the year, but especially around the holidays!

1 env. active dry yeast
1/4 c. warm water
1 c. warm milk
1/4 c. shortening
1-1/4 c. sugar, divided
1 t. salt

1 egg, lightly beaten
3-1/2 to 3-3/4 c. all-purpose
   flour
1 T. orange zest
1/2 c. butter, melted

In a small bowl, dissolve yeast in very warm water, about 110 to 115 degrees. In a large bowl, mix milk, shortening, 1/4 cup sugar, salt and egg. Add yeast mixture; blend well. Stir in enough flour to form a soft dough. Knead dough on a lightly floured surface until smooth and elastic, about 6 to 8 minutes. Place in a greased bowl, turning once to grease top. Cover; let rise in a warm place until dough is double in size, about one hour. Punch dough down; divide in half. Roll each half into a 15-inch by 10-inch rectangle. In a bowl, combine orange zest, remaining sugar and butter. Spread half of orange zest mixture on each rectangle. Roll up dough jelly-roll style, starting with one long edge. Cut into one-inch slices. Arrange in 2 greased 11"x7" baking pans. Cover and let rise until double, about 45 minutes. Bake, uncovered, at 375 degrees for 20 to 25 minutes, until golden. Spread Glaze over warm rolls. Makes 30.

Glaze:

2 c. powdered sugar
1 t. butter, softened

1/4 c. whipping cream
1/2 t. lemon extract

In a bowl, combine all ingredients.

Bacon curls make a festive and tasty breakfast plate garnish. Just fry bacon until it's browned, but not crisp. Immediately roll up slices and fasten each with a toothpick.

Pumpkin Spice Coffee Cake

Sharon Copeland
Seymour, TX

This cake, along with a fresh pot of coffee, is just perfect for sharing with family & friends on those special holiday mornings.

18-1/4 oz. pkg. spice cake mix
2 eggs, beaten
1/2 c. water
1/2 t. baking soda

15-oz. can pumpkin
8-oz. container frozen whipped
   topping, thawed
Garnish: cinnamon, nutmeg

In a bowl, combine dry cake mix, eggs, water, baking soda and pumpkin. With an electric mixer on medium speed, beat for 2 minutes. Pour into 3 greased 8" round cake pans or one greased 13"x9" baking pan. Bake at 350 degrees for 20 to 25 minutes, until a toothpick tests clean when inserted into cake's center. Allow to cool; spread with whipped topping and sprinkle with cinnamon and nutmeg. Cover and refrigerate. Serves 10 to 12.

Cinnamon Roll Cake

Shiloh Swanson
Fairbanks, AK

I created this recipe several years ago and knew it was a hit when my husband and his friends devoured almost the whole thing within 15 minutes of it coming out of the oven!

18-1/2 oz. pkg. yellow cake mix
1 c. brown sugar, packed
1 T. cinnamon

2 c. powdered sugar
1/4 c. milk
1-1/2 t. vanilla extract

Prepare cake mix according to package directions; spread half the batter in a greased 13"x9" baking pan. In a small bowl, stir together brown sugar and cinnamon. Sprinkle evenly over batter. Top with remaining batter. Run a table knife through the layers to create swirls. Bake at 350 degrees for 30 to 35 minutes, until a toothpick inserted into the center comes out clean. In a bowl, combine powdered sugar, milk and vanilla, adding more milk if needed to reach desired consistency. Spread over warm cake. Cut into squares to serve. Serves 10.

Cozy Christmas
Brunch

Blueberry French Toast Bake
Darlene Harzler
Marshallville, OH

My sister-in-law makes this yummy dish each year for our Christmas brunch. It's the first thing I put on my plate!

12 slices day-old white bread, crusts trimmed
2 8-oz. pkgs. cream cheese, cubed
2 c. blueberries, divided
1 doz. eggs, beaten

2 c. milk
1/3 c. maple syrup
1 c. sugar
2 T. cornstarch
1 c. water
2 t. butter

Cut bread into cubes; spread in a greased 13"x9" baking pan. Top with cream cheese and one cup blueberries. In a bowl, combine eggs, milk and syrup; pour over blueberries. Cover with aluminum foil; refrigerate at least 30 minutes before baking. Bake, covered, at 350 degrees for 30 minutes. Remove foil; bake for 30 minutes longer, or until golden. In a saucepan over medium heat, combine sugar, cornstarch and water; bring to a boil. Boil 3 minutes, stirring constantly. Stir in remaining blueberries. Reduce heat; simmer for 8 to 10 minutes, until berries burst. Stir in butter; serve blueberry syrup over individual servings. Serves 8 to 12.

An easy and fun addition to your brunch table...mini cinnamon buns! Start with a tube of refrigerated cinnamon rolls; unroll the dough strips, cut in half lengthwise and sprinkle with more cinnamon and sugar. Roll the strips into one-inch buns; place in a well-greased mini muffin tin and bake as directed. Allow to cool slightly; remove from tins while still warm.

Chocolate-Maple Muffins

Jennifer Millett
Mechanicsville, VA

My son loves these and would eat them for every meal if he could.
They're good for breakfast and sweet enough for dessert.

1 c. all-purpose flour
1 t. baking powder
1/2 t. baking soda
1/4 t. salt
2 T. sugar
2/3 c. buttermilk

2-1/2 T. maple syrup
1 egg, beaten
2 T. butter, melted and cooled
  slightly
1 c. mini semi-sweet chocolate
  chips

Grease a 12-cup muffin tin or a 24-cup mini muffin tin. In a large bowl, combine flour, baking powder, baking soda, salt and sugar. In a separate bowl, combine buttermilk, syrup, egg and butter. Add buttermilk mixture to flour mixture; stir well. Fold in chocolate chips. Fill muffin cups 2/3 full. Bake at 350 degrees for 10 to 12 minutes for regular muffins, or 7 to 9 minutes for mini muffins. Makes one to 2 dozen.

Snickerdoodle Muffins

Lana Rulevish
Ashley, IL

These muffins go as fast as you can make them!

1 c. butter, softened
2 c. sugar, divided
2 t. vanilla extract
2 eggs
2-1/4 c. all-purpose flour

3/4 t. baking powder
3/4 t. baking soda
3/4 t. cream of tartar
1-1/4 c. sour cream
2 T. cinnamon

In a bowl with an electric mixer on medium speed, beat butter and one cup sugar until fluffy, about 3 minutes. Add vanilla and eggs, one at a time; beat well. In a separate bowl, combine flour, baking powder, baking soda and cream of tartar. Add flour mixture and sour cream alternately to butter mixture. In a shallow bowl, combine remaining sugar and cinnamon. Using an ice cream scoop, scoop batter and drop into cinnamon-sugar; coat well. Place in greased muffin cups. Bake at 350 degrees for 20 to 22 minutes. Makes 12 to 15.

Cozy Christmas Brunch

Loaded Cinnamon Rolls

Toni Radunz
Oklahoma City, OK

I make these cinnamon rolls with my children on the weekends. They love them.

1 loaf frozen bread dough,
    thawed
1 c. brown sugar, packed
1 T. cinnamon

6 T. butter, softened
1/3 c. raisins
1/3 c. walnuts

Roll out thawed dough on a lightly floured surface to form a 15-inch by 7-inch rectangle. In a small bowl, combine brown sugar and cinnamon; set aside. Spread butter over dough. Sprinkle cinnamon-sugar mixture, raisins and walnuts over butter. Starting at one long edge, roll up dough jelly-roll style. Cut roll into 16 slices. Divide rolls between 2 lightly buttered 9" round cake pans. Set aside in a warm place and allow dough to rise until double in size, about one hour. Bake at 400 degrees for 15 minutes, or until golden. Frost warm rolls with Cream Cheese Frosting. Makes 16.

Cream Cheese Frosting:

1/2 c. butter, softened
1 c. powdered sugar
1/3 c. cream cheese, softened

1 t. cinnamon
1 t. vanilla extract

In a bowl, combine all ingredients. Beat with an electric mixer on medium speed until fluffy.

A vintage canning jar filled with delicious homemade preserves makes a thoughtful hostess gift. Tie on a topper of colorful holiday fabric and ribbon.

Spiced Nut Scones

JoAnn

The spicy scent of these scones baking in the oven immediately brings Christmas to mind.

3 c. buttermilk biscuit
   baking mix
1/4 c. sugar, divided
1/2 t. cinnamon
1/8 t. nutmeg

1/2 c. walnuts, coarsely chopped
3 eggs, divided
1/3 c. milk
Garnish: butter, preserves

In a bowl, combine baking mix, 3 tablespoons sugar, cinnamon, nutmeg and walnuts. With a fork, blend in 2 eggs and milk. On a lightly floured baking sheet, use wax paper to press dough into a 1/2-inch thick, 11-inch circle. In a small bowl, beat remaining egg; brush over dough. Sprinkle with remaining sugar. Cut dough into 12 wedges; arrange wedges about 1/4 inch apart. Bake at 400 degrees for 12 minutes, or until golden. Serve warm with butter and preserves. Makes one dozen.

Eggnog Quick Bread

Angie Biggin
Lyons, IL

This moist holiday bread also makes great French toast the next day!

2-1/2 c. all-purpose flour
2 t. baking powder
1/2 t. salt
1/4 t. nutmeg
2 eggs, beaten
1 c. sugar

1 c. eggnog
1/2 c. butter, melted and cooled
   slightly
1 t. vanilla extract
Optional: 1/2 t. rum or rum
   extract

In a large bowl, combine flour, baking powder, salt and nutmeg. In a separate bowl, combine remaining ingredients. Add egg mixture to flour mixture; stir until just moistened. Batter will be lumpy. Pour into a buttered and floured 9"x5" loaf pan. Bake at 350 degrees for 40 to 45 minutes, until a toothpick inserted in the center comes out clean. Cool in pan on a wire rack. Makes one loaf.

Chill-Chasing Soups & Breads

Christmas Eve
Pasta e Fagioli

Karen Crooks
West Des Moines, IA

I often prepare this tummy-warming soup for our Christmas Eve dinner. It's quick & easy, yet hearty enough to satisfy our hunger after church services.

3/4 lb. ground beef chuck
1 onion, chopped
1 T. oil
2 cloves garlic, minced
1 stalk celery, chopped
1 carrot, peeled and chopped
1 T. dried basil
1 T. dried oregano

15-oz. can diced tomatoes
4 c. chicken broth
15-oz. can Great Northern
   beans, drained and rinsed
1 c. ditalini pasta, uncooked
Garnish: shredded Parmesan
   cheese

In a large heavy soup pot over medium heat, brown beef and onion in oil until beef is no longer pink; drain. Stir in garlic, celery and carrot; cook for 4 minutes. Sprinkle with basil and oregano. Stir in tomatoes with juice and chicken broth; bring to a boil. Reduce heat and simmer for 30 minutes. Stir in beans and pasta; simmer for 6 to 7 minutes, or until pasta is cooked. Ladle into bowls; garnish individual servings with Parmesan cheese. Serves 4 to 6.

Because the rest of our family lives out of town, on Christmas Day we get up early, open gifts, have our special breakfast and enjoy the whole day in our pajamas! We spend the day playing games received, doing puzzles and just enjoying each other's company. One of my fondest memories is seeing my husband, Frank, sitting at the kitchen table, playing "Pretty, Pretty Princess" with our 4-year-old daughter. He had earrings, bracelets and rings dangling off him. Even now the thought of Daddy in the jewelry brings back special memories!

–Maxine Rendulic, Dayton, OH

Chill-Chasing Soups & Breads

Cynthia's Zuppa Toscana

*Cynthia Dodge
Layton, UT*

We love going to our favorite Italian restaurant, but our budget doesn't always allow for it. I came up with this simple alternative to the restaurant version. My family thinks this one's even better!

4 14-oz. cans chicken broth
14-oz. can beef broth
16-oz. container whipping cream
6 to 8 potatoes, peeled and
    sliced
1 lb. spicy ground pork sausage,
    browned

1 lb. ground pork sausage,
    browned
1/4 t. red pepper flakes
1/4 t. salt
1/4 t. pepper
1 bunch fresh kale, coarsely
    chopped

In a large Dutch oven, add broths and whipping cream. Cook over low heat, stirring often, until nearly boiling. Add potatoes, sausage and seasonings; continue to cook over low heat for 40 minutes, or until potatoes are tender. Remove from heat; add kale. Cover; let stand for 5 minutes, or until kale is wilted. Serves 4 to 6.

Fresh kale can be found in your market's produce section. To prepare, lay rinsed kale flat on a cutting board. Run a sharp knife along the stem; discard stem. Coarsely chop or tear kale into half dollar-size pieces.

Velvet Broccoli-Cheese Soup

Faye Saterfield
Monroe, LA

This soup is easy to make and perfect for feeding a crowd. I brought it to a Christmas dinner at work, and it was such a hit...everyone was asking if I had any more!

16-oz. pkg. frozen broccoli cuts
10-oz. can diced tomatoes with
   green chiles, drained
2 T. dried parsley
1 t. dried thyme
1 t. salt

1/4 c. milk
16-oz. pkg. pasteurized process
   cheese spread, cubed
Garnish: shredded cheese,
   croutons or oyster crackers

In a large soup pot over medium heat, cook broccoli according to package directions until crisp-tender; drain. Add tomatoes with juice, seasonings and milk; stir well. Reduce heat to a simmer. Add cheese; cover and simmer, stirring occasionally, until cheese melts. Garnish as desired. Serves 4 to 6.

Winter Artichoke Soup

Karren Bates
Trophy Club, TX

My friends Lucile and Barb served this soup at one of our winter garden club meetings and everyone raved over it!

1 lb. Italian ground pork
   sausage
2 28-oz. cans Italian-style plum
   tomatoes
2 14-oz. cans artichoke hearts,
   drained and chopped

1-oz. pkg. onion soup mix
3 c. water
1/2 t. dried oregano
1/2 t. dried basil

In a Dutch oven over medium heat, brown sausage; drain. Add tomatoes with juice and remaining ingredients; stir well. Bring to a boil. Reduce heat; stir and simmer for 20 minutes, or until heated through. Serves 6 to 8.

❧ *Chill-Chasing* ☙
Soups & Breads

Wynter's Potato-Fennel Soup
Wynter Nichols
Marina, CA

I love the taste of fresh fennel! This zesty soup is a great way to introduce fennel to people who may never have tried it.

2 bulbs fennel, trimmed
   and chopped
1 onion, chopped
8 cloves garlic, chopped
6-1/2 c. chicken broth
juice of 1 lemon

3 potatoes, peeled and diced
1 pt. half-and-half
1 lb. mild Italian ground pork
   sausage, browned
1 T. fennel or anise seed, toasted
6 to 7 t. Greek seasoning

Place fennel, onion and garlic in a baking pan sprayed with non-stick vegetable spray. Bake, uncovered, at 350 degrees for 30 to 45 minutes, until fennel is tender. In a soup pot over high heat, bring broth to a boil. Add fennel mixture, lemon juice and potatoes. Simmer until potatoes are tender, 15 to 20 minutes. Remove from heat. Using an immersion blender, process soup until smooth. Stir in half-and-half, sausage, seed and seasoning. Return to heat; simmer until heated through. Serves 8 to 10.

A snowy winter afternoon is the perfect time to browse seed and plant catalogs and start planning your flower and vegetable gardens for spring.

Cheesy Lasagna Soup

Amiee Gess
Washington, ME

This is the perfect soup for a cold winter night...warm, cheesy and filling. It's also a great way to get my kids to eat some spinach!

1 lb. Italian turkey sausage
  links, casings removed
2 c. onion, chopped
4 cloves garlic, minced
2 c. sliced mushrooms
4 c. chicken broth
15-oz. can Italian-seasoned
  diced tomatoes

15-oz. can tomato sauce
1 c. bite-size mafalda pasta,
  uncooked
2 c. fresh spinach, chopped
1 c. shredded mozzarella cheese
1/4 c. grated Parmesan cheese
Garnish: 4 t. fresh basil, sliced

In a soup pot over medium heat, crumble sausage and cook until no longer pink; drain. Add onion, garlic and mushrooms; cook and stir until tender. Add broth, tomatoes with juice and tomato sauce. Bring to a boil; add pasta. Simmer until pasta is just barely tender, about 11 minutes; stir in spinach and cheeses. Remove from heat; allow to cool. Garnish individual servings with basil. Serves 6.

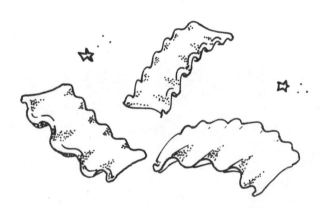

Mafalda pasta is a flat wide ribbon pasta that looks like tiny lasagna noodles! If you can't find mafalda pasta for Cheesy Lasagna Soup, use a similar-size pasta like bowtie or rotini.

Belle's Yeast Rolls

Belle Perry
Lawrenceburg, KY

Everyone looks forward to my homemade yeast rolls every Christmas.
I always add a special touch...a pat of butter nestled in each one.

2 envs. active dry yeast
3 c. warm water
2/3 c. sugar
2 eggs, beaten

1 T. salt
1 c. shortening, melted
8 to 9 c. all-purpose flour

In a large bowl, dissolve yeast in very warm water, about 110 to
115 degrees; add remaining ingredients. Mix well. Let stand until
dough doubles in bulk, at least one hour. Knead dough for about
5 minutes, or until no longer sticky. On a lightly floured surface, roll
out dough 1/4-inch thick; cut into 20 squares. Place on ungreased
baking sheets; allow to rise again, at least one hour. Bake at
450 degrees for 10 to 15 minutes, until golden. Makes 20.

Every year, about a week before Christmas, our family gets
together and makes "gingerbread" houses, but we use graham
crackers instead. We collect all sorts of candies and decorative
icings to use, and use vanilla icing for the "glue." Even though
most of our children are married, we still get together every
year for this occasion...now the grandchildren enjoy
our family tradition!

–Tina George, El Dorado, AR

Christmas Croissants

Laurie Ellithorpe
Argyle, NY

This recipe is oh-so easy! It was given to me many years ago...one of the hundreds of recipes I have collected over the years.

2 envs. active dry yeast
1 c. warm water
5 c. all-purpose flour, divided
1/3 c. sugar
1-1/2 t. salt
1/4 c. butter, melted and cooled
   slightly

3/4 c. evaporated milk
2 eggs, divided
1 c. chilled butter
1 T. water

In a large bowl, dissolve yeast in very warm water, 110 to 115 degrees; let stand 5 minutes. In a separate bowl, combine one cup flour, sugar and salt. Add to yeast mixture; stir. Add melted butter, milk and one egg; beat until smooth. To a separate large bowl, add remaining flour; cut in chilled butter until mixture is crumbly. Add yeast mixture; mix well but do not knead. Cover; refrigerate overnight. Punch down dough. Turn out onto a lightly floured surface. Knead about 6 times and divide into 4 pieces. On a floured surface, roll out each piece into a 16-inch circle; cut each circle into 8 wedges using a pizza cutter. Roll up wedges beginning at the wide end; place point side-down, 3 inches apart, on ungreased baking sheets. Curve ends to form a crescent. Cover and let rise in a warm place for one hour. Beat remaining egg with water; brush over rolls. Bake at 325 degrees for 20 to 25 minutes, until lightly golden. Makes 32.

To accurately measure flour, first use a spoon to fluff up the flour while it's still in the container. Then, spoon flour into your measuring cup and level with a knife. This method prevents extra flour from being packed into your measuring cup when you scoop it directly from the container.

Chill-Chasing
Soups & Breads

Nana's Slovak Christmas Eve Soup

Nancy Rossman
Port Richey, FL

This wonderful recipe is from my grandmother who was from Czechoslovakia. I remember going on Sunday drives throughout the year, picking mushrooms and then stringing them with a needle and thread. Nana would hang them by the stove to dry.

1 onion, chopped
1 T. butter
15-oz. can sauerkraut
6 c. water
3 c. mushrooms, chopped

1 clove garlic, pressed
1 t. pepper
1 t. paprika
14-oz. Kielbasa sausage ring, diced and browned

In a large saucepan over medium heat, sauté onion in butter. Add undrained sauerkraut and remaining ingredients except sausage. Increase heat to medium-high and bring to a boil, stirring often. Add sausage; reduce heat to low. Cover and simmer for one hour, adding water if needed. Serve soup ladled over bowls of Homemade Noodles. Serves 6 to 8.

Homemade Noodles:

4 c. all-purpose flour
1/8 t. salt

1 egg, beaten
1 to 2 t. water as needed

In a large bowl, combine flour, salt and egg; mix in just enough water to moisten through. Knead dough until smooth, adding more flour if needed. Divide dough in half. On a well-floured surface, roll out dough very thinly. With a sharp knife, cut into 4-inch wide strips. Dust strips with flour to prevent sticking; stack the strips. Cut each stack into one-inch wide strips; cut again into 1/2-inch squares. Transfer noodles to a large pot of boiling water; cook until noodles float to the top. Drain; rinse in cool water.

Turn Christmas cards into festive napkin rings. Cut them into strips with decorative-edge scissors, join ends with craft glue and add a sprig of faux holly...simple!

4-Way Versatile Quick Bread
Tracee Cummins
Amarillo, TX

This recipe is perfect for gift-giving. It's fast and easy, and you can choose the flavor to suit the recipient. It can also be made without any additions for a sweet, plain bread that's good for toasting.

3 eggs
1-1/2 c. sugar
2/3 c. oil

2-1/2 c. all-purpose flour
3-1/2 t. baking powder
1 t. salt

Grease and flour the bottom only of a 9"x5" loaf pan. In a bowl, beat eggs with an electric mixer on high speed until foamy. Add sugar and oil; beat until creamy. Add remaining ingredients; beat on low speed until blended. Pour batter into pan. Bake at 350 degrees for one hour and 10 minutes, or until a toothpick inserted in the center tests clean. Makes one loaf.

Fresh Apple:

1 t. vanilla extract
2 c. apples, peeled, cored and
  diced

1/2 c. sugar
1-1/2 t. apple pie spice

Add vanilla to basic batter. Toss apples with sugar and spice. Pour half the batter into loaf pan; top with half the apple mixture. Repeat layers, ending with apples. Bake as directed above.

Harvest Pumpkin:

15-oz. can pumpkin
1 T. pumpkin pie spice

1 t. vanilla extract

Add pumpkin, spice and vanilla to basic batter; blend well. Bake as directed above.

Delicious Cranberry:

2 c. sweetened dried cranberries
1/3 c. orange juice

1 t. vanilla extract
1/2 t. nutmeg

Add all ingredients to basic batter; blend well. Bake as directed above.

46

Sweet-and-Sour Cabbage Soup

Michelle Brodman
Southfield, MI

This is one soup everyone will eat. Let it simmer on the stovetop all day long...the longer, the better!

1 head cabbage, chopped
1 onion, chopped
4 cloves garlic, pressed
2 carrots, peeled and shredded
1 T. olive oil
28-oz. can diced tomatoes
29-oz. can tomato sauce
1 bay leaf
1 t. dill weed
salt and pepper to taste
1 lb. beef short ribs
1-1/2 c. sugar
1 c. vinegar

In a large stockpot over medium heat, sauté cabbage, onion, garlic and carrots in oil for about 15 minutes. Add tomatoes and tomato sauce; stir well. Stir in seasonings. Add enough water to cover vegetables; bring mixture to a boil. Add short ribs; return to a boil. Add sugar and vinegar: mix well. Reduce heat; simmer for about 2 hours. Allow to cool; skim fat. If time allows, refrigerate overnight to skim solidified fat more easily. After refrigeration, return to a boil; reduce heat and simmer for several hours more, if desired. Discard bay leaf before serving. Serves 12.

Uncertain whether your yeast is still good? Place one teaspoon yeast into a cup of very warm water and add one tablespoon of sugar. If the yeast foams and rises in 10 minutes, it is still good for baking.

Seafood Stew

Crystal Branstrom
Russell, PA

This stew is so good on a cold winter day. Serve with a crisp salad and a loaf of hot, crusty Italian bread.

2-1/2 c. chicken broth
1/2 c. long-cooking rice, uncooked
2 t. chili powder
2 cloves garlic, minced
14-1/2 oz. can diced tomatoes, drained
2-1/4 c. green, red and yellow peppers, thinly sliced

1/2 c. onion, thinly sliced
1/2-lb. fillet orange roughy, cut into bite-size pieces
1/4 lb. frozen cooked medium shrimp, thawed
3/4 c. orange juice concentrate

In a saucepan over high heat, bring broth to a boil. Add rice, chili powder and garlic. Stir well; return to a boil. Reduce heat; cover and simmer for 15 to 20 minutes, until rice is tender. Add tomatoes, peppers and onion. Cover; cook over medium heat until vegetables are tender. Add fish, shrimp and orange juice. Cover; simmer over low heat for 2 to 4 minutes, until fish flakes easily with a fork and shrimp are heated through. Serves 4.

When I was a girl traveling with my family on Christmas Eve, our car got stuck in a snow bank late at night as we were driving home from Ohio. A lovely Amish couple graciously welcomed us into their home, and we spent the night with them. When we arrived home on Christmas Day, to our amazement, our presents were tucked neatly under the tree! It took my sisters and I years to find out that a friend of the family had set them out for us.

—Jodi Schnetzler, Three Rivers, MI

Chill-Chasing
Soups & Breads

Quick Mediterranean Soup

Jennifer Niemi
Nova Scotia, Canada

Really quick, really easy and really tasty. Although this recipe is perfect for a casual family meal, it's also easily dressed up with some freshly baked bread and a glass of white wine for company.

3 c. onion, finely chopped
1/4 c. olive oil
8 c. vegetable broth, divided
4 to 5 cloves garlic, minced
10-oz. pkg. frozen chopped
   spinach, thawed and drained

28-oz. can diced tomatoes
2-1/4 t. sugar
4-1/2 t. dried basil
1/4 t. pepper
1 c. orzo pasta, uncooked

In a large saucepan over medium heat, sauté onion in oil until tender, about 10 minutes. Add 4 cups broth and remaining ingredients except orzo. Cover and simmer for 20 minutes. Stir in orzo and remaining broth. Cover; simmer for an additional 10 minutes, or until orzo is tender. Serves 8.

Poppy Seed-Cheese Bread

Francie Stutzman
Clinton, OH

This is so good served with soup or a salad...or both!

1 onion, chopped
1/2 c. butter, melted
2 T. poppy seed

1/8 t. salt
1 loaf French bread
1 lb. Swiss cheese, thinly sliced

In a skillet over medium heat, sauté onion in butter until tender. Stir in poppy seed and salt. Place bread on a sheet of aluminum foil. Score loaf at 1/2-inch intervals, but do not cut all the way through. Place a slice of Swiss cheese into each cut. Drizzle butter mixture over top. Wrap bread tightly in foil. Bake at 350 degrees for 30 minutes, or until bread is crisp and cheese is melted. Slice before serving. Serves 8.

Just Plain Muffins

Judy Swoboda
College Station, TX

*These muffins are a favorite in our family. They're good with jam
and butter, or even just plain...hence the name! My mother got this
recipe from her mother in 1931. I still have the original note that my
grandmother sent to my mother with the recipe included.*

2 c. all-purpose flour	1 egg, beaten
2 T. baking powder	1/2 c. evaporated milk
1/4 c. sugar	1/2 c. water
1/2 t. salt	2 T. shortening

In a large bowl, mix flour, baking powder, sugar and salt; stir in
remaining ingredients one at a time. Spray a 12-cup muffin tin with
non-stick vegetable spray; fill muffin cups 2/3 full. Bake at 350 degrees
for 30 minutes, or until golden. Makes one dozen.

For a special holiday presentation, chill bottled
beverages in a bucket of frozen cranberries
instead of ice cubes.

Chill-Chasing Soups & Breads

Oriental Chicken Soup

Sandra Sullivan
Aurora, CO

We enjoy this quick chicken soup on busy weekday evenings. The whole process takes just 20 minutes for homemade soup, and it's yummy and healthy!

3 14-1/2 oz. cans chicken broth
2 c. water
1 T. fresh ginger, peeled and grated
1 clove garlic, slivered
1/4 to 1/2 t. red pepper flakes
8-oz. pkg. whole-wheat spaghetti, uncooked and divided

2 boneless, skinless chicken breasts, thinly sliced
1 red pepper, thinly sliced
1 c. snow peas, chopped
juice of 1 lime
2 green onions, thinly sliced
salt to taste

In a large soup pot over high heat, bring broth, water, ginger, garlic and red pepper flakes to a boil. Add half of the spaghetti, reserving remainder for a future use. Reduce heat; simmer until spaghetti is tender, about 6 to 8 minutes. Add chicken, pepper and snow peas; simmer until chicken is fully cooked, about 3 minutes. Stir in lime juice, green onions and salt. Serves 4.

Every year when I was small, my parents took my sisters and me out to eat on Christmas Eve. When we arrived home after dinner, Santa had always stopped by while we were at the restaurant. So, we always opened our gifts on Christmas Eve, which gave us more time on Christmas morning to spend at my grandparents' house. It was a wonderful way to spend Christmas, with less stress for my parents. I still remember the year that we got home and a helicopter was flying over our house...all I could see was a red blinking light. I swore it was Rudolph's nose, and since the gifts were waiting under the tree when we walked inside, there was no convincing me otherwise!

–Cathy Zeltner, Northwood, OH

Easy Oatmeal Rolls

Nancy Girard
Chesapeake, VA

This is an often-requested recipe! I put the dough ingredients in my bread machine and let the machine do the work, but this version calls for doing it by hand. Either way, it's easy and yummy.

1 T. active dry yeast
1 c. warm water
1/4 c. sugar
1-1/2 t. salt
1/2 c. quick-cooking oats or old-
  fashioned oats, uncooked

1 egg, beaten
3 T. oil
3 c. bread flour, divided
Garnish: 1 to 2 T. butter

In a large bowl, dissolve yeast in very warm water, about 110 to 115 degrees. Add sugar, salt, oats, egg, oil and 2-1/4 cups flour; mix well. Turn onto a lightly floured surface; knead in remaining flour for several minutes. Return dough to bowl; let rise in a warm place for one to 1-1/2 hours. Punch down; divide and shape dough into golfball-sized balls. Arrange in a greased 13"x9" baking pan. Cover; let rise about one hour. Bake at 350 degrees for 20 to 25 minutes. While rolls are still warm, spread butter over tops. Makes 15 to 18.

Potato Biscuits

Susan Willie
Ridgecrest, NC

These biscuits are wonderful with any meal.

2-1/2 c. biscuit baking mix
1/3 c. margarine, softened
1/2 c. milk

1 c. mashed potatoes or mashed
  sweet potatoes

In a bowl, mix all ingredients until a soft dough forms. Turn dough onto a surface lightly dusted with additional baking mix. Gently roll to coat. Shape into a ball; knead 3 or 4 times. Roll out dough 1/2-inch thick. Cut with a 2-inch biscuit cutter dipped in baking mix. Arrange on an ungreased baking sheet. Bake at 450 degrees for 10 to 12 minutes, until golden. Makes 8 to 10.

Chill-Chasing Soups & Breads

Bean & Turkey Soup

Robin Werner
Dysart, IA

*After enjoying a few too many holiday indulgences, I created
this simple, healthy recipe...my family loves it!*

2 lbs. ground turkey
1 onion, chopped
1/2 lb. carrots, peeled and
   chopped
32-oz. container chicken broth
16-oz. can black beans, drained
   and rinsed
16-oz. can kidney beans,
   drained and rinsed

16-oz. can navy beans, drained
   and rinsed
16-oz. can Great Northern
   beans, drained and rinsed
salt, pepper and cayenne pepper
   to taste

In a large stockpot over medium heat, brown turkey; drain. Remove
turkey to a separate bowl. In the same pot, sauté onion and carrots
until soft. Return turkey to stockpot along with remaining ingredients.
Simmer over medium-low heat for 2 to 3 hours, stirring occasionally.
Makes 6 to 8 servings.

Twisty bread sticks are a tasty go-with for soup. Brush refrigerated
bread stick dough with a little beaten egg and dust with Italian
seasoning, then pop 'em in the oven until toasty. Yummy!

Sweet Southern Cornbread
Brandie Skibinski
Salem, VA

I love any kind of cornbread, but my favorite has to be sweet cornbread. It is moist, delicious and a perfect side to any dinner!

1/2 c. sugar
2 T. honey
1 egg, beaten
1/4 c. butter, melted and cooled
   slightly
1/2 c. milk

1/2 c. water
1 c. yellow cornmeal
1 c. all-purpose flour
1-1/2 t. baking powder
1/2 t. salt

In a large bowl, whisk together sugar, honey, egg, butter, milk and water. In a separate bowl, combine remaining ingredients. Slowly stir cornmeal mixture into sugar mixture until well combined. Batter may be a little lumpy. Pour into a greased 8"x8" baking pan. Bake at 350 degrees for about 15 to 20 minutes, until a toothpick inserted in the center comes out clean. Cut into squares to serve. Serves 8.

Mama's Southern Hushpuppies
Cora Phillips
Ozark, AL

This recipe was handed down from my mama...it's the only one she ever used. These are a yummy side served with fried catfish!

1 c. white cornmeal
1/2 c. all-purpose flour
1-1/2 to 2 T. sugar
1 t. salt
2 T. baking powder
3/4 c. buttermilk

1 egg, beaten
1 onion, chopped
Optional: 1 jalapeño pepper,
   chopped and seeds removed
peanut oil for frying

In a large bowl, combine cornmeal, flour, sugar, salt and baking powder. Add remaining ingredients except oil. Mixture will be thick but should not be dry. If dry, add a little more buttermilk. Heat a deep fryer of peanut oil to 350 degrees. Carefully drop batter from a small spoon. Fry in small batches until dark golden on all sides. Drain on paper towels. Serves 8 to 10.

Burger Barley Soup

Lori Rosenberg
University Heights, OH

*In our family, the first batch of this soup signals
the arrival of cooler weather.*

1-1/2 lbs. lean ground beef
28-oz. can diced tomatoes
8-oz. can tomato sauce
1/2 c. catsup
6 c. water
2 c. carrots, peeled and sliced
1-1/2 c. onion, chopped

1-1/2 c. celery, chopped
1/2 c. green pepper, chopped
1/2 c. pearl barley, uncooked
1 T. beef bouillon granules
1 T. salt
1/8 t. pepper
2 bay leaves

In a Dutch oven over medium heat, brown beef until no longer pink; drain. Remove beef from pot; rinse in a colander. Return beef to pot; stir in tomatoes with juice and remaining ingredients. Bring to a boil. Reduce heat; cover and simmer for one hour, or until vegetables and barley are tender. Remove bay leaves before serving. Serves 10 to 12.

Decorate a jar of homemade preserves in an instant with a paper muffin cup liner in a festive holiday design. Simply flatten the liner and place it design-side up on top of the jar, pressing it down around the lid. Tie in place with a narrow ribbon or jute.

Buffalo Chicken Soup

Kristi Bestwick
Butler, PA

This slow-cooker recipe is perfect for those cold days when you just can't get warm. This soup is guaranteed to warm you up from the inside out! I use a rotisserie chicken to speed up the process.

6 c. milk
3 10-3/4 oz. cans cream of
   chicken soup
3 c. cooked chicken, shredded
1 c. sour cream

1/4 to 3/4 c. hot pepper sauce,
   to taste
2 T. ranch salad dressing mix
Optional: shredded Cheddar
   cheese

Combine all ingredients in a 5-quart slow cooker; stir well. Cover and cook on low setting for 4 to 5 hours. If desired, garnish individual servings with cheese. Serves 12 to 15.

Lori's Kid-Friendly Chili

Pat Beach
Fisherville, KY

My daughter left this recipe for me to make while I was babysitting. The kids were so excited to come home from school to a big bowl of their mother's chili.

1 lb. ground beef
14-1/2 oz. can petite diced
   tomatoes
10-oz. can diced tomatoes with
   green chiles
15-oz. can tomato sauce

15-1/2 oz. can mild chili beans
1-1/4 oz. pkg. mild chili
   seasoning mix
2 c. water
8-oz. pkg. thin spaghetti,
   uncooked and divided

In a Dutch oven over medium heat, brown beef; drain. Add both cans of tomatoes with juice, tomato sauce, chili beans, seasoning mix and water. Bring to a boil. Reduce heat; simmer over low heat for 30 minutes. While chili is simmering, break half the spaghetti into thirds and cook as directed on package, reserving the rest for a future use. Drain but do not rinse spaghetti. Add spaghetti to pot. Continue to simmer for another 5 minutes, until chili thickens slightly. Serves 8 to 10.

Jason's Favorite Pea Soup

Stormy Snow
Branson, MO

My son has loved this hearty pea soup recipe since he was young.
I like to serve it with ham sandwiches for a complete meal.

16-oz. pkg. dried split peas
2 14-1/2 oz. cans low-sodium
   chicken broth
1/2 c. water
1/2 c. celery, chopped
1/4 t. garlic powder
1/4 t. dried marjoram

1/4 t. dried thyme
1/8 t. pepper
1/2 to 3/4 lb. cooked ham, diced
1 potato, peeled and diced
2 to 3 carrots, peeled and diced
salt to taste
Optional: 1/2 c. whipping cream

In a Dutch oven, cover peas with broth and water. Over medium-high
heat, bring to a boil; boil for 2 minutes. Remove from heat; cover and
let stand for one hour. Return to stovetop; add celery and seasonings.
Return to a boil; cover, reduce heat to low and simmer for 2 hours,
stirring occasionally. Add an additional cup of water if needed. Add
ham, potato and carrots. Simmer for 45 minutes, stirring occasionally.
Add salt to taste. For a creamier texture, stir in cream during the last
15 minutes of cooking time. Serves 6 to 8.

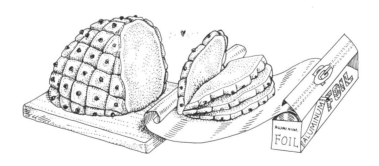

A budget-friendly source for cooked ham...ask for the end cuts at
the deli counter. Ends too small to return to the slicer are often
sold at a reduced price. Just remove the casings and dice!

Southwest Butternut Squash Soup

Arden Regnier
East Moriches, NY

When my husband and I got tired of eating Thanksgiving leftovers a few years ago, I decided to make soup with our leftover butternut squash. The result was so scrumptious that I've repeated it several times since! If you're not using leftovers, one large squash should do the trick.

4 c. butternut squash, cooked
    and mashed
1/2 c. brown sugar, packed
1 jalapeño pepper, diced and
    seeds removed
1 stalk celery, finely diced

1/2 onion, finely diced
1 t. oil
salt and pepper to taste
2 c. chicken broth
12-oz. can evaporated milk
ground cumin to taste

Mix squash with brown sugar; set aside. In a soup pot over medium heat, sauté jalapeño pepper, celery and onion in oil until tender. Add salt, pepper, broth and squash mixture. Using an immersion blender, purée mixture until smooth, or purée in small batches in a blender and return to pot. Stir in milk and cumin; cover and simmer about 15 minutes. Cook, uncovered, for an additional 15 minutes, stirring occasionally, until soup thickens slightly. Serves 6.

If a recipe calls for cooking a dish covered in the oven or on the stovetop for a long, low simmer, it can probably be converted to a slow-cooker recipe. Two to 4 hours of stovetop or oven cooking time will convert to 4 to 6 hours in the slow cooker on high, or 7 to 9 hours on low. Layer root vegetables under meat and reduce the amount of liquid and seasonings used. Adjust seasonings toward the end of cooking time, if needed.

Soups & Breads

Chicken Poblano Chowder

Margie Slentz
Denver City, TX

This recipe always gets wonderful reviews, and I've shared it with an abundance of people. There's just enough heat to make it so satisfying on a cold winter's day. If there happen to be any leftovers, they freeze well.

3 carrots, peeled and diced
2 onions, diced
5 stalks celery, chopped
2 T. garlic, minced
2 to 3 poblano peppers, chopped
   and seeds removed
1 t. salt
1/2 t. pepper
1/2 t. ground cumin
1/4 t. dried thyme

2 T. olive oil
12 c. chicken broth
3 c. cooked boneless, skinless
   chicken breast, diced
11-oz. can corn, drained
1/2 c. butter
1/2 c. all-purpose flour
1/2 t. hot pepper sauce, or
   to taste
1 c. whipping cream

In a soup pot over medium heat, sauté carrots, onions, celery, garlic, peppers and seasonings in oil, until vegetables are tender. Add broth; cook until carrots are tender. Stir in chicken; cook, stirring often, until mixture begins to thicken, about 30 minutes. Add corn; remove from heat. In a large skillet over medium heat, melt butter. Add flour; cook and stir for 3 to 4 minutes, just until flour is golden. Ladle one cup of hot liquid from the stockpot into skillet, whisking constantly. Pour mixture from the skillet into the stockpot, stirring to blend. Return soup pot to heat and cook 3 to 5 minutes longer, until mixture thickens. Remove from heat; stir in hot sauce and cream. Serves 12 to 16.

A loaf of sourdough bread is a tasty partner for a hearty pot of chowder...pick up a ready-made loaf at the market and pop it in the oven for a crisp, warm crust!

Sweet Potato-Corn Chowder

Gail Wright
Bellflower, MO

*This is a very tasty chowder that I love to make in the fall
and winter. It's ready to serve in about an hour.*

14-oz. pkg. Kielbasa sausage
  ring, diced
1 c. onion, chopped
1 T. garlic, minced
3 T. all-purpose flour
1-1/2 t. ground cumin
1-1/2 t. chili powder
6 c. chicken broth

16-oz. pkg. frozen corn
2 c. sweet potatoes, peeled
  and cubed
3/4 lb. boneless, skinless,
  chicken breasts, chopped
1 c. whipping cream
1 t. pepper

In a Dutch oven over medium heat, brown sausage for 5 minutes,
stirring occasionally. Add onion and garlic. Cook and stir for 5 minutes.
Stir in flour, cumin and chili powder. Cook and stir for 2 minutes
longer. Stir in chicken broth; bring to a boil. Add corn, sweet potatoes
and chicken; return to a boil. Reduce heat and simmer, covered, for
about 20 minutes, or until sweet potatoes are tender and chicken is
cooked through. Stir in cream and pepper; heat through. Serves 8 to 10.

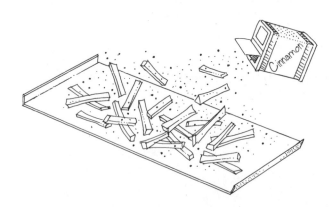

Homemade sweet potato chips...yummy! Peel sweet potatoes,
slice thinly, toss with oil and spread on a baking sheet.
Place on the center oven rack and bake at 400 degrees
for 22 to 25 minutes, turning once. Sprinkle with
cinnamon-sugar and serve warm.

Chill-Chasing
Soups & Breads

Fiesta Bubble Bread

Amy Hunt
Traphill, NC

This is fabulous on the Christmas Eve dinner menu.
A little spicy and loaded with cheesy goodness.

1/2 c. butter, melted
1-1/2 c. shredded Mexican-
blend cheese
1/4 c. shredded mozzarella
cheese

10-oz. jar sliced jalapeño
peppers, drained
1 t. dried parsley
2 12-oz. tubes refrigerated
biscuits, cut into quarters

In a large bowl, combine butter, cheeses, pepper slices and parsley; add biscuits and toss to coat. Transfer to an ungreased Bundt® pan. Bake at 350 degrees for 30 minutes, or until golden. Invert onto a serving plate; serve warm. Serves 8.

Herby Bubble Bread

Suzy McNeilly
Colfax, WA

This is a perfect bread to bring to a potluck or serve with soup. If you're looking for extra oomph, shake in some red pepper flakes!

3 1-lb. loaves frozen bread
dough, thawed but still
chilled
1/4 c. olive oil
3 T. Italian salad dressing mix

1 c. shredded sharp Cheddar
cheese
1 t. garlic, minced
1 red onion, finely chopped

Cut dough into one-inch cubes; place in a large bowl. Pour remaining ingredients over top. Using your hands, toss until dough cubes are coated. Place mixture in a greased 13"x9" baking pan. Place in a warm area; cover and let rise until double in size. Bake at 350 degrees for 20 to 25 minutes, until golden. Serves 6 to 8.

Make veggie or bean soups creamier without adding extra cream...simply purée a cup or two of the soup in a blender, then stir it back into the soup pot.

Mexi-Cheese Soup

Trisha Donley
Pinedale, WY

This soup is fabulous served with a grilled sandwich.

1/4 c. butter
1/2 c. onion, chopped
1 clove garlic, minced
1/2 c. all-purpose flour
1/2 t. ground cumin
1/2 t. salt
1/8 t. pepper
4 c. milk

1-1/2 c. chicken broth
4-oz. can diced green chiles
14-1/2 oz. can fire-roasted diced
    tomatoes
1 c. shredded Cheddar cheese
1 c. shredded Monterey Jack
    cheese

In a Dutch oven over medium heat, melt butter. Sauté onion and garlic until tender. Add flour and seasonings; stir and cook for one minute. Add milk and broth; stir well and simmer for 5 minutes. Add chiles and tomatoes with juice; bring to a boil. Remove from heat. Stir in cheeses; let stand until melted. Makes 8 servings.

Quickly turn a group of mismatched tag-sale candleholders into a shimmering set...spray them all your favorite color of craft paint. Shades of white and ivory look snowy tucked in among evergreens and holiday decorations.

Holiday Posole

Sue Moak
Menard, TX

One tradition many in the Southwest look forward to on Christmas Eve is a steamy bowl of posole (pronounced po-SO-lay). It's a spicy corn stew that was an ancient ceremonial dish meant to celebrate life's blessings. Serve with cornbread or tortillas.

2 center-cut pork chops, cubed
2 t. canola oil
1 c. onion, chopped
3/4 c. green pepper, chopped
1 to 2 cloves garlic, minced
1-1/2 T. ground red chili pepper
 or paprika
1 t. ground cumin
1 T. dried oregano
salt and pepper to taste

14-1/2 oz. can chicken broth
5-1/2 c. water
8-oz. can tomato sauce
15-1/2 oz. can yellow hominy,
 drained and rinsed
14-1/2 oz. can diced tomatoes
juice of 1/2 lime
Optional: chopped fresh cilantro,
 sour cream, shredded cheese

In a large soup pot over medium heat, brown pork in oil. Add onion, green pepper and garlic; sauté until tender. Stir in seasonings. Add broth, water and tomato sauce. Cover and cook until pork is tender, about 45 minutes. Stir in hominy, tomatoes with juice, lime juice and cilantro, if using. Bring to a boil; reduce heat and cover. Simmer for 15 minutes longer. Garnish individual servings with sour cream and shredded cheese, if desired. Serves 4 to 6.

Sing we all merrily Christmas is here,
The day we love best of all days in the year.
Bring forth the holly, the box and the bay,
Deck out our cottage for glad Christmas day.

–Old English Poem

Swiss Whipped Cream Nut Loaf

Nancy Babinec
Parma, OH

This was my grandmother's recipe. I was always afraid to try it because I thought it wouldn't live up to my memories of how good the bread tasted. Thank goodness I was wrong! Both the delicious taste and the fond memories have been preserved.

1 c. golden raisins
1 c. boiling water
1 c. whipping cream
1 egg, beaten
1 c. sugar

1 c. chopped walnuts
1-3/4 c. all-purpose flour
1-1/2 t. baking powder
1/4 t. salt

Place raisins in a small bowl; cover with water. Let stand for 15 minutes. Drain on paper towels; pat dry. Meanwhile, beat cream in a bowl with an electric mixer on low speed. Gradually increase speed to medium; beat until very soft peaks form. Add egg and sugar; beat until well blended. Stir in walnuts and raisins. In a separate bowl, blend remaining ingredients; stir into cream mixture. Grease a 9"x5" loaf pan on the bottom only; pour in batter. Bake at 325 degrees for one hour and 10 minutes, or until a toothpick inserted in the top of loaf comes out clean. Cool for 15 minutes in pan on a wire rack; remove from pan and cool completely before serving. Serves 10 to 12.

Soup suppers are a fuss-free way to get together with friends, neighbors and extended family. Set up a buffet table, decorate simply with holly and greenery and it's all set. Each family brings a favorite soup to share, along with the recipe. What a delicious way to try a variety of soups and maybe find a new favorite!

Chill-Chasing
Soups & Breads

German Fresh Apple Bread

Abi Buening
Grand Forks, ND

Our family loves to eat quick breads and muffins for breakfast during the holiday season.

1/2 c. shortening
1 c. plus 1 T. sugar, divided
2 eggs, beaten
1 c. apples, peeled, cored and
    finely chopped
1-1/2 T. milk

1/2 t. vanilla extract
1 c. all-purpose flour
1 t. baking soda
1/2 t. salt
1-3/4 t. cinnamon, divided
1 c. chopped nuts

In a large bowl, beat shortening and one cup sugar; add eggs and mix well. Stir in apples, milk and vanilla. In a separate bowl, mix flour, baking soda, salt and 1/2 teaspoon cinnamon; add to shortening mixture, mixing well. Fold in nuts. Spoon into a greased 9"x5" loaf pan. Combine remaining sugar and cinnamon; sprinkle over top. Bake at 350 degrees for 50 minutes to one hour, until a toothpick inserted into center of loaf tests clean. Makes one loaf.

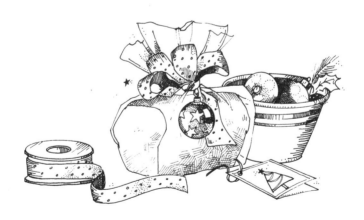

A loaf of homemade fruit bread is always a welcome gift!
Make sure it stays fresh and tasty...let the bread cool completely
before wrapping well in plastic wrap or aluminum foil.

Potato-Leek Soup

Mary Fountain
Ontario, Canada

A scrumptious slow-cooker meal...if you like your soup really, really creamy, definitely add the evaporated milk.

6 slices bacon, chopped
2 leeks, chopped
3 10-1/2 oz. cans chicken broth
3 c. water
5 potatoes, peeled and diced
1 c. carrot, peeled and diced
1 c. celery, diced
1/2 t. salt

1/2 t. white pepper
1/2 t. dill weed
1/2 c. all-purpose flour
2 c. half-and-half
Optional: 12-oz. can evaporated
  milk
Garnish: shredded Cheddar
  cheese

In a large, deep skillet over medium-high heat, cook bacon and leeks until bacon is crisp and leeks are soft. Drain. Transfer bacon and leeks to a slow cooker; stir in broth, water, vegetables and seasonings. Cover and cook on low setting for 6 to 7 hours, stirring occasionally. During the last 30 minutes of cooking time, in a small bowl, whisk together flour and half-and-half. Stir into the slow cooker along with evaporated milk, if using. Cover and cook an additional 30 minutes. Garnish individual servings with shredded cheese. Serves 6.

Help your children share the giving spirit of Christmas. Before the holidays, go through their toys with them, pulling out two or three they no longer play with. After they've been cleaned, donate them to a shelter or community project.

Chill-Chasing
Soups & Breads

Corn & Shrimp Chowder
Vickie

This hearty and satisfying soup will warm you up on a chilly winter evening!

2 onions, sliced
2 T. butter
16-oz. pkg. frozen corn, divided
3 potatoes, peeled and cubed
4 c. chicken broth

1 bay leaf
1-1/2 c. half-and-half
1/2 lb. small shrimp, peeled
   and cleaned
Garnish: minced fresh parsley

In a stockpot over medium heat, sauté onions in butter until tender. In a blender, process half the corn until fine; add to stockpot. Add remaining corn, potatoes, broth and bay leaf to stockpot. Simmer until potatoes are tender. Add half-and-half; heat through. Just before serving, add shrimp. Cook for 3 to 4 minutes, until shrimp are pink and cooked through. Discard bay leaf. Sprinkle individual servings with parsley before serving. Serves 4 to 6.

Apple "Cider" Soup
John & Anne Newsome
Columbia, SC

This soup tastes like a cup of hot apple cider...however, the chicken broth and five-spice powder add an interesting twist! It's refreshing served between courses of a dinner party.

3 c. chicken broth
4 c. apple juice
1/2 t. cider vinegar
1/2 t. Chinese five-spice powder
1 Gala apple, peeled, cored and
   diced

1 Granny Smith apple, peeled,
   cored and diced
1/8 t. salt
red pepper flakes to taste

In a saucepan over medium heat, combine broth, apple juice, vinegar and five-spice powder. Bring to a slow simmer. Add apples; simmer until apples are just tender. Stir in salt and red pepper flakes. Serves 8 to 10.

Mom's Lefse

Heather Garthus
Newfolden, MN

My mom has been making lefse, a soft traditional Norwegian bread, during the holidays since I was a little girl. Now I've started making it for my family.

10 lbs. redskin potatoes, peeled
1/2 c. butter, melted
1/2 c. whipping cream
1 T. salt
4 c. all-purpose flour

In a large stockpot over high heat, cover potatoes with water and cook until tender; drain. Run hot potatoes through a potato ricer; transfer 8 cups to a large bowl. Add butter, cream and salt; mix well and let cool to room temperature. Stir in flour, one cup at a time, until a soft dough forms. Pinch off pieces of dough and form into walnut-sized balls. On a lightly floured surface, flatten balls to 1/8-inch thick. Cook on a hot lightly greased griddle until bubbles form; flip and cook other side until golden. Place on a dampened tea towel to cool slightly; cover with another tea towel until ready to serve. Makes about 4 dozen.

Colonial Brown Bread

Jennie Gist
Gooseberry Patch

This bread is best served warm, but don't worry...it reheats well!

4 c. whole-wheat flour
1-1/3 c. all-purpose flour
1 c. brown sugar, packed
4 t. baking soda
1 t. salt
4 c. buttermilk

In a large bowl, combine all ingredients except buttermilk. Add buttermilk; mix well. Divide batter between 2 greased 9"x5" loaf pans. Bake at 350 degrees for one hour, or until a toothpick tests clean. Serve warm; refrigerate leftovers. Makes 2 loaves.

Caroling Party Supper

Snowy-Day Chicken Casserole
Marilyn Morel
Keene, NH

This is a favorite comfort food during the winter. The nutmeg and sherry give it a special touch. My boys love this dish after playing in the snow or building snowmen. I serve it with hot crusty rolls and buttered carrots.

1/2 c. butter, divided
1/4 c. all-purpose flour
1-1/2 c. chicken broth
1 c. sour cream
1/2 c. onion, diced
2 stalks celery, diced
1/8 t. nutmeg
salt and pepper to taste
1/4 c. dry sherry or chicken
   broth

8-oz. pkg. flat egg noodles,
   cooked
6 boneless, skinless chicken
   breasts, cooked and cubed
1 c. soft bread crumbs
1/2 c. shredded Parmesan
   cheese

In a saucepan over medium heat, melt 1/4 cup butter; whisk in flour. Add broth and sour cream; stir until thick. Add onion, celery, nutmeg, salt and pepper. Remove from heat; stir in sherry or broth. Place noodles in a lightly greased 13"x9" baking pan. Cover with chicken; pour butter mixture over top. In a bowl, melt remaining butter; toss with bread crumbs. Sprinkle crumbs and Parmesan cheese over top. Bake, uncovered, at 350 degrees for 35 minutes, or until bubbly. This casserole can be made a day ahead of time and refrigerated overnight. Serves 8.

A festive touch for your holiday table...a wreath of rolls! Arrange thawed dinner rolls in a ring on a parchment paper-lined baking sheet. Brush with butter, sprinkle with green herbs and bake as directed. So pretty on a cake stand!

Caroling Party Supper

Swiss Alps Casserole

Pam Enebrad
Beaufort, SC

I created this recipe to duplicate a dish our family enjoyed while we were living in Switzerland. We lived in a mountain village that specialized in making its own sausage. Family & friends love it!

5 potatoes, peeled and cubed
14-oz. pkg. Kielbasa sausage
   ring, sliced
1 onion, chopped
Optional: 1 to 2 slices bacon,
   chopped

1 c. penne pasta, cooked
8-oz. pkg. shredded Gruyère or
   Swiss cheese

In a large saucepan, cover potatoes with water and boil until tender; drain and set aside. In a skillet over medium-high heat, brown sausage, onion and bacon, if using; drain. Combine all ingredients; transfer to a 13"x9" baking pan that has been sprayed with non-stick vegetable spray. Bake, uncovered, at 350 degrees for 30 minutes, or until cheese is melted. Serves 4 to 6.

Popcorn ball ornaments...so tasty, they may not make it to the tree! Using a skewer, poke a small hole into the top of a 3-inch popcorn ball. Snap the end off a mini candy cane to create a point, and gently press the sharp end of the cane into the popcorn ball far enough to make a loop. Fill a pastry bag with frosting and use frosting to "glue" mini candies to the ball.

Impossible Tex-Mex Chicken Pie

Carol McKeon
Lebanon, TN

Our family loves spicy foods, probably because my mother was Spanish and notably the best cook in the family. Using the basic impossible pie ingredients, I came up with this easy-to-prepare dish. It disappears very quickly so it must be a "hot" and tasty item!

2 c. cooked chicken, cubed
14-1/2 oz. can fire-roasted diced
   tomatoes, drained
11-oz. can sweet corn & diced
   peppers, drained
4-oz. can diced green chiles,
   drained

1/2 c. buttermilk biscuit baking
   mix
1 c. evaporated or regular milk
2 eggs, beaten
1/2 c. shredded Cheddar cheese
Garnish: sour cream, guacamole

In a bowl, combine chicken, tomatoes, corn and chiles. Spread evenly in a 9" pie plate that has been sprayed with non-stick vegetable spray. In a separate bowl, blend baking mix, milk and eggs. Spoon over chicken mixture; sprinkle with cheese. Bake at 400 degrees for 35 to 40 minutes, until a knife tip inserted in the center comes out clean. Garnish with sour cream and guacamole. Serves 6.

For old-fashioned farmhouse charm, group together an assortment of vintage tin graters on a tabletop or mantel, tuck a tea light under each and enjoy their cozy flickering lights.

Caroling Party Supper

Chile Rice Casserole

Debra Clark
La Mirada, CA

I've been making this easy recipe for so many years, I don't even remember where I first got it. I usually end up making a double batch when my family gets together.

2 c. cooked white rice
2 c. sour cream
8-oz. pkg. shredded Colby Jack
   cheese

4-oz. can diced green chiles,
   drained
salt and pepper to taste
Optional: 4 t. butter

In a bowl, combine all ingredients except butter. Transfer to a 8"x8" baking pan that has been sprayed with non-stick vegetable spray. If desired, dot with butter. Bake, uncovered, at 350 degrees for 30 minutes. Serves 6 to 8.

When my husband and I were first married and had little money, we shopped for a nativity scene after Christmas. We found one with a music box that played "Silent Night." When our children were very young we began a tradition of displaying the nativity on Thanksgiving Day. They took turns unwrapping each figure with squeals of excitement, but Baby Jesus stayed in the box until Christmas Eve. The nativity remained the focus of attention for the month leading up to Christmas. They enjoyed rearranging the animals and figures and winding the music box and singing "Silent Night." My grandchildren have shared the same tradition even though Joseph is missing his nose, the camel's head is glued on and the original angel had to be replaced. We too have aged and changed through the years, but this tradition remains timeless!

–Sharon Laney, Maryville, TN

Red Flannel Spaghetti

Paula Marchesi
Lenhartsville, PA

Ever since the slow cooker came into my house, I have more time to do the things I love to do! I've been making this spaghetti for more than 40 years, but the slow cooker has simplified it. You'll love this out-of-this-world delicious sauce.

1 lb. ground beef
1 lb. ground pork
3/4 lb. sweet Italian sausage
    links, sliced
4 onions, finely chopped
8 cloves garlic, minced
2 14-1/2 oz. cans diced
    tomatoes
2 14-1/2 oz. cans stewed
    tomatoes
4 6-oz. cans tomato paste
1/2 c. water

1/4 c. Worcestershire sauce
2 T. brown sugar, packed
1 T. olive oil
1/4 c. fresh parsley, minced
2 t. dried basil
1 t. dried oregano
1 t. dried sage
1/2 t. dried marjoram
1/2 t. salt
1/2 t. pepper
4 bay leaves
16-oz. pkg. spaghetti, uncooked

In a Dutch oven, cook beef, pork, sausage, onion and garlic over medium heat until meat is no longer pink; drain. Transfer to a 5-quart slow cooker. Stir in remaining ingredients except spaghetti. Cover and cook on low setting for 8 hours, or until hot and bubbly. Discard bay leaves before serving. Prepare spaghetti according to package instructions; drain. To serve, ladle sauce over bowls of hot spaghetti. Makes 12 servings.

A big pot of spaghetti & meatballs is a delightful, budget-friendly meal for a casual get-together with friends. Just add warm garlic bread, a big tossed salad and plenty of paper napkins!

Caroling Party Supper

Florentine Meatballs

Carol Van Rooy
Ontario, Canada

A yummy way to get your kids to eat their spinach.

10-oz. pkg. frozen spinach,
   thawed and drained
1-1/3 lbs. ground turkey
1 onion, finely diced
3 cloves garlic, minced
1 egg, beaten

1/4 c. milk
3/4 c. dry bread crumbs
1/2 c. grated Parmesan cheese
salt and pepper to taste
2 to 3 T. oil

In a large bowl, combine all ingredients except oil; mix well. Form into 12 to 16 balls. Arrange on a rimmed baking sheet; drizzle with oil. Bake at 400 degrees for 20 to 25 minutes, until cooked through. Serves 4.

Homestyle Pot Roast

Karen Crosby
Myrtle Beach, SC

An absolutely delicious pot roast...and so easy to fix!

1/4 c. all-purpose flour
2/3 c. water
1-oz. pkg. onion soup mix
3 to 4-lb. beef rump roast

4 redskin potatoes, quartered
1 onion, quartered
16-oz. pkg. baby carrots
Optional: chopped fresh parsley

Shake flour in a roasting bag; place bag in a 13"x9" baking pan. Add water and soup mix to bag; squeeze bag to combine with flour. Add roast to bag; turn bag to coat roast with flour mixture. Place potatoes, onion and carrots in bag around roast. Close bag with provided nylon tie; cut six, 1/2-inch slits into top of bag. Tuck ends of bag into pan. Bake at 325 degrees for 2 hours, or until roast reaches desired doneness, about 140 to 145 degrees on a meat thermometer for medium. Sprinkle with parsley before serving, if desired. Serves 6 to 8.

A smiling face is half the meal.

–Latvian proverb

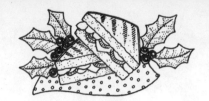

Brazilian Rice & Beans

Jamie Guimaraes
Pittsburgh, PA

My husband was born in Brazil, and he calls this rice & beans recipe a "contemporary twist to an age-old Brasilian favorite." We love making this hearty dish for guests.

1 lb. ground beef
8 to 10 slices bacon, chopped
2 T. butter
3 T. onion, chopped
2 cloves garlic, minced
1 c. long-cooking rice, uncooked
2 c. boiling water

1 t. salt
2 15-oz. cans black beans,
　drained and rinsed
15-1/2 oz. can chili beans
3/4 c. beef gravy
1/3 c. Worcestershire sauce
1/2 c. barbecue sauce

In a large skillet over medium-high heat, brown beef and bacon until very well browned and crisp; drain and set aside. In a saucepan over medium heat, melt butter; sauté onion and garlic until tender. Add uncooked rice; stir to coat. Pour boiling water over top; add salt and cover with lid. Simmer, covered, until all water is absorbed and rice is tender, about 15 minutes. Return skillet to heat; add beans and remaining ingredients. Simmer, covered, about 5 minutes, or until flavors blend and mixture is heated through. Serve beef mixture over warm rice mixture. Serves 3 to 4.

Make an ice wreath to hang from your outdoor tree branches...it will look so pretty sparkling in the sun! Just place greenery and some fresh cranberries inside a round gelatin mold, add about two inches of water and freeze. Fill the rest of the mold with water and freeze again. Remove wreath from mold and hang from a length of jute.

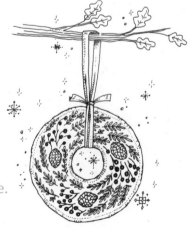

Caroling Party Supper

Pepper Steak

Paulette Alexander
Newfoundland, Canada

This is one of my mother's recipes. It's a tasty dish for potluck gatherings. It also freezes well.

1 onion, chopped
1 t. oil
2 cubes beef bouillon
1 c. hot water
14-1/2 oz. can diced tomatoes
1 lb. stew beef, cubed
1/2 green pepper, diced
2 to 3 stalks celery, diced

10-oz. can sliced mushrooms, drained
1/2 t. pepper
1/2 t. dried basil
1/2 t. garlic powder
1 t. soy sauce
cooked rice

In a skillet over medium-high heat, cook onion in oil until tender. Dissolve bouillon cubes in hot water and add to onion. Add tomatoes with juice and remaining ingredients except rice. Cover and simmer over low heat, stirring occasionally, for 2 to 3 hours, until beef is tender. Serve over cooked rice. Serves 4 to 6.

Our favorite new tradition is having our young niece visit from San Diego. She comes to Kansas to spend Thanksgiving with us, and delights in decorating our Christmas tree on Thanksgiving Day. In the past, our tree has always been very color-coordinated and "proper." Now, we give her free rein to do whatever she wants with it. She has even used ornaments that we had forgotten were stored away in the basement, each with some very special memories attached. She has helped us remember that Christmas is about making memories, not about having a "perfect" tree!

–Janice Spillane, Abilene, KS

Baked Pork Chops

Constance Spilman
Fredericktown, OH

This is an original recipe from my mother, Virginia. It's a family favorite. My brother always requests this when he comes to visit from Florida. Serve it with cooked rice and be sure to spoon the sauce over everything. Yum!

4 pork chops
1/3 c. celery, diced
1/2 t. salt
1/4 t. pepper
2 T. brown sugar, packed

2 T. lemon juice
15-oz. can tomato sauce
1/2 c. water
1/2 t. mustard

In a greased skillet over medium heat, brown chops on both sides, but do not cook through. Transfer to an ungreased 8"x8" baking pan. Sprinkle with celery, salt and pepper. In a bowl, mix remaining ingredients; pour over top. Cover pan with aluminum foil; bake at 350 degrees for one hour, or until chops are cooked through and tender. Makes 4 servings.

Do your favorite slow-cooker recipes finish cooking a few hours before you get home? If your slow cooker doesn't have a timer setting, then you may want to prepare the ingredients the night before. If you refrigerate the filled crock overnight, it will take 2 to 3 hours longer to cook, which is perfect when you will be out & about all day!

Caroling Party Supper

Hoppin' John

Caroline Weinert
Bedford, IN

It's said that eating Hoppin' John on New Year's Day will bring a prosperous year filled with luck. The black-eyed peas are symbolic of pennies or coins. This is an easy dish that my family really enjoys!

1 c. dried black-eyed peas
8 c. water
6 slices bacon, chopped
3/4 c. onion, diced

1 clove garlic, minced
1 c. long-cooking rice, uncooked
2 t. salt
1/4 t. pepper

Cover peas with water and soak 8 hours to overnight; rinse and drain. Add 8 cups water to a large saucepan; bring to a boil. Add peas; boil for 2 minutes. Remove from heat; cover and let stand for one hour. Drain peas, reserving 6 cups of cooking water. In a Dutch oven over medium-high heat, cook bacon until crisp; remove from pan, reserving drippings. Drain bacon on paper towels. Add onion and garlic to Dutch oven; cook for one to 2 minutes, until tender. Stir in peas, rice, seasonings and reserved cooking water; bring to a boil. Cover and reduce heat. Simmer for one hour, stirring occasionally, until peas and rice are tender. Stir in bacon before serving. Serves 4 to 6.

Sauerkraut & Pork

Phyllis Hoth
Pleasant Hill, IA

Eating sauerkraut at holiday gatherings is a tradition in my family, and even my grandchildren love it! What a wonderful aroma fills the house. I have always associated it with love.

2 32-oz. jars sauerkraut
1 to 2 potatoes, peeled and
    grated

1 to 2-lb. pork loin roast

In a Dutch oven, combine undrained sauerkraut and potatoes. Place pork loin on top; spoon some sauerkraut mixture over pork. Bake, covered, at 350 degrees for 5 to 6 hours, or until pork is fully cooked and fork-tender. Serves 8 to 10.

Ginger-Panko Fried Chicken

Laurel Perry
Loganville, GA

Any leftovers reheat well and they're just as good!

2 c. oil	1 t. ground ginger
1 egg	1/2 t. garlic powder
1/2 c. milk	salt and pepper to taste
1 c. panko bread crumbs	4 boneless, skinless chicken
3 T. brown sugar, packed	breasts

Heat oil in a large skillet or electric frying pan. In a shallow bowl, beat egg with milk. In a separate shallow bowl, combine panko crumbs, brown sugar and seasonings. Coat each chicken breast thoroughly in egg mixture, then dredge in panko crumb mixture. After coating each chicken breast, stir panko crumb mixture. Gently place chicken in hot oil. Cook for about 4 minutes on each side, or until crust is golden and chicken juices run clear when pierced. Drain on paper towels. Makes 4 servings.

A sweet cookie cutter wreath for your kitchen...no gluing required!
On a flat surface, arrange cutters into a circular shape; clip
together with silver paper clips. Carefully flip wreath over;
secure the same spots on the other side. Tie with lengths
of ribbon for extra security.

Caroling Party Supper

Easiest Baked Mac & Cheese

Cristi Aulbach
Hartford City, IN

My very best friend Maudlyn gave me this easy recipe for baked mac & cheese. You just mix all the ingredients together, pop it in the oven and forget about it until it's done. It is so creamy and good. You'll never make mac & cheese any other way again!

2-1/4 c. water
2 c. elbow macaroni, uncooked
1/4 c. butter

16-oz. container sour cream
2 c. shredded Cheddar cheese

In a saucepan over high heat, bring water to a boil. In a greased 13"x9" baking pan, stir together uncooked macaroni, butter, sour cream and cheese. Pour boiling water over top; stir to combine. Bake, uncovered, at 375 degrees for 45 minutes. Serves 4 to 6.

Delight your family by dressing up a weeknight meal of
mac & cheese...spoon it into individual ramekins before baking.
Why not spread out your favorite Christmas tablecloth
and get out your fancy stemware too?

Mexican Baja Quiche

Laurel Liebrecht
Yakima, WA

This is one of my family's very favorite dishes. Whenever the kids came home from college, it was the first meal they requested. I always make two at a time...and there are no leftovers!

9-inch pie crust
1-1/2 c. shredded Monterey
 Jack or Pepper Jack cheese,
 divided
16-oz. can refried beans
1/2 to 1 lb. Italian or chorizo
 ground pork sausage,
 browned

2 eggs, beaten
1-1/2 c. sour cream
hot pepper sauce to taste
1/2 t. salt
2 T. diced green chiles, drained
Optional: sliced avocado and
 tomato

Place pie crust in a deep 9" quiche pan or pie plate, forming to fit pan. Sprinkle one cup of cheese over crust. Spoon refried beans over top; sprinkle with sausage. In a small bowl, whisk together eggs, sour cream, hot sauce and salt. Pour egg mixture over ingredients in pie crust. Top with remaining cheese and green chiles. Bake at 325 degrees for one hour to 75 minutes, until set. Let stand 5 minutes before slicing. Top with slices of avocado and tomato, if desired. Serves 8.

Tuck silverware into clean, brightly colored mittens at each place setting. Use a scarf as a table runner for a warm wintertime gathering.

Caroling Party Supper

Ham & Egg Fried Rice

Karen Ensign
Providence, UT

Growing up in a Taiwanese family, this was something my mom made whenever we had leftover rice. Now my kids enjoy it too!

3 T. oil, divided
2 eggs, beaten
1/2 c. carrot, peeled and
   shredded
1/2 c. cooked ham, diced

1 c. frozen peas, thawed
1 green onion, finely sliced
3 c. cooked rice
salt or soy sauce to taste

Heat a wok over high heat for 30 seconds. Swirl in one tablespoon oil; immediately reduce heat to medium. Add eggs, stirring to cook just until set. Remove eggs to a bowl; break up with a fork. Heat remaining oil in wok over high heat for 30 seconds. Add carrot; cook and stir for one minute. Reduce heat to medium. Add ham, peas, onion and rice; cook and stir for 2 to 3 minutes, until heated through. Season with salt or soy sauce. Return eggs to pan; heat through. Serves 4.

Coconut-Lime Fish Fillets

Jocelyn Medina
Phoenixville, PA

A little taste of the tropics...nice in the middle of winter.

1 lime, halved
4 red snapper or salmon fillets
3 cloves garlic, minced
1 onion, chopped
1 stalk celery, diced

2 T. olive oil
1/2 c. canned coconut milk
1/2 c. salsa
cooked rice

Squeeze lime juice over fish fillets; set aside. In a skillet over medium heat, sauté garlic, onion and celery in oil until tender. Stir in coconut milk and salsa. Simmer for 10 minutes, stirring occasionally. Add fillets, skin-side up, gently pushing them into the sauce. Simmer for 5 to 10 minutes, until fish flakes easily with a fork. Transfer fillets to a serving platter; keep warm. Continue to cook sauce in skillet over low heat until it thickens. Ladle some sauce over fillets; serve any remaining sauce on the side with cooked rice. Serves 4.

Cindy Lou Who Hash

Cindy Linthicum
Baltimore, MD

I made up this dish one night when I had some browned meat to use and potatoes in the freezer. We were getting ready to watch "How the Grinch Stole Christmas," and my husband dubbed this recipe Cindy Lou Who Hash. Cornbread makes a nice side.

1 lb. ground turkey or beef
32-oz. pkg. frozen diced
   potatoes, thawed

16-oz. jar salsa
2 c. shredded Cheddar cheese

In a skillet over medium heat, brown meat until no longer pink; drain. Add potatoes; cook, stirring occasionally, until golden. Add salsa; stir and simmer for 15 to 20 minutes. Stir in cheese, 1/2 cup at a time, until cheese melts. Serves 5.

Thanksgiving Meatloaf

Carolyn Gourley
Duncannon, PA

It's all the delicious flavors of a holiday meal in one tasty dish!

12-oz. pkg. herb-flavored
   stuffing mix, crushed
2 lbs. ground turkey
2 eggs, beaten

16-oz. can whole-berry
   cranberry sauce
12-oz. jar turkey gravy

In a large bowl, combine crushed stuffing mix with turkey and eggs; mix well. Pat half the turkey mixture into a 9"x5" loaf pan. Spoon cranberry sauce over top. Press remaining turkey mixture over sauce. Bake, uncovered, at 350 degrees for one hour, or until cooked through. Serve slices with gravy. Serves 6.

To mix up a no-mess meatloaf, place all the ingredients in a large plastic zipping bag. Seal the bag and squish it until everything is well combined...then just toss the empty bag!

Caroling Party Supper

Carrie's Turkey Moussaka

Caroline Pacheco
Stafford, VA

Traditionally moussaka calls for beef or lamb, but I thought it would be fun to try ground turkey breast. This is a fantastic, healthy meal that my family loves.

2 eggplants, thinly sliced
1 T. olive oil
2 onions, thinly sliced
1 t. garlic, minced
1 lb. ground turkey
14-1/2 oz. can diced tomatoes

2 T. fresh parsley, chopped
salt and pepper to taste
2 eggs, beaten
2 5.3-oz. containers plain Greek
  yogurt
1 T. grated Parmesan cheese

In an ungreased non-stick skillet over medium heat, brown eggplant slices on both sides; remove from skillet and set aside. Add oil; sauté onions and garlic for 2 minutes. Add turkey; cook and stir until browned. Drain. Add tomatoes with juice, parsley, salt and pepper. Bring to a boil; reduce heat and simmer for 20 minutes, or until turkey is tender. Arrange half the eggplant slices in an ungreased 13"x9" baking pan. Top with turkey mixture, followed by remaining eggplant slices. In a bowl, combine eggs, yogurt and additional salt and pepper. Pour over eggplant slices; sprinkle cheese over top. Bake, uncovered, at 350 degrees for 45 minutes, or until golden, bubbly and eggplant is tender. Serves 8 to 10.

Santa's little helpers will enjoy cutting out designs from last year's Christmas cards. Even easier...use a large craft punch! Once they're cut, glue onto store-bought cards for handmade gift tags that add charm to every package.

Kentucky Hot Browns

Melissa Knight
Athens, AL

My mother and I made these open-faced sandwiches day after Christmas to use up our leftover turkey. There's just something special about Christmas in my home state of Kentucky!

6 thick slices white bread
6 slices deli roast turkey breast
1 lb. bacon, crisply cooked

3 plum tomatoes, sliced
1 c. shredded Parmesan cheese

Preheat broiler; place bread slices on an ungreased baking sheet. Broil for one to 2 minutes. Top bread slices with slices of turkey and bacon; broil for another 4 to 5 minutes. Serve topped with tomato slices, Mornay Sauce and Parmesan cheese. Makes 6 servings.

Mornay Sauce:

1/2 c. butter
1/3 c. all-purpose flour
3-1/2 c. milk

1/2 c. shredded Parmesan
    cheese
salt and pepper to taste

Melt butter in a large saucepan over medium heat; stir in flour and whisk for one minute. Gradually stir in milk; bring to a boil and cook, whisking constantly, until thickened. Before serving, whisk in Parmesan cheese, salt and pepper.

Sandwiches are a tasty solution when family members will be dining at different times during the busy holiday season. Fix sandwiches ahead of time, wrap 'em individually in aluminum foil and refrigerate. Pop them into a toaster oven or under a broiler to heat...fresh, full of flavor and ready whenever you are!

Caroling Party Supper

Mom's Famous Potato Salad
Christina Mamula
Aliquippa, PA

This was Mom's specialty. She made it only during the holidays. At times, I think we were more excited about her potato salad at Christmas than the gifts from Santa.

6 to 7 lbs. potatoes, peeled
   and cubed
1 doz. eggs, hard-boiled, peeled
   and chopped
1-1/2 c. celery, chopped
1 c. onion, chopped
2 t. vinegar

2-1/2 c. mayonnaise-type salad
   dressing
2-1/2 T. mustard
2 t. dill pickle juice
3/4 c. sugar
1/3 c. milk

In a large stockpot over high heat, cover potatoes with water and bring to a boil. Cook for 20 to 25 minutes, until potatoes are tender. Drain, but do not rinse. Transfer potatoes to a large serving bowl; allow to cool. Add eggs, celery and onion. In a separate bowl, whisk together remaining ingredients. Pour over potato mixture; mix well. Cover and chill before serving. Serves 10 to 12.

Save a step by boiling eggs and potatoes at the same time!
Let the potatoes cook in a large pot of boiling water for about
10 minutes, then add the eggs and cook for another
15 minutes. Remove from heat; drain.

Chicken Pizzaiola

Sharon Velenosi
Costa Mesa, CA

A yummy Italian dish that's really easy to make! Serve with a side of spaghetti, if you wish.

2 lbs. chicken breasts and thighs
4 potatoes, peeled and quartered
1 onion, sliced
15-oz. can green peas, drained
16-oz. can whole button
    mushrooms, drained

28-oz. can diced tomatoes
salt and pepper to taste
1 t. dried oregano
1/4 c. grated Parmesan cheese
1/4 c. olive oil

Arrange chicken, potatoes, onion, peas and mushrooms in a roasting pan. Pour tomatoes with juice over top. Sprinkle with salt, pepper, oregano and Parmesan cheese; drizzle with oil. Cover tightly with aluminum foil; bake at 375 degrees for one hour and 15 minutes, or until chicken juices run clear when pierced with a fork. Serves 4.

One of my most memorable Christmases took place in the early '60s, when I was ten years old. When I opened my Christmas gifts, I saw the most fabulous Barbie doll ever made! She was so fashionable with her three wigs. Another package held beautiful clothes for her. My little sister Lisa, who was three years old, said with delight, "Momma made your Barbie clothes and she let me play with her while you were at school!" It appears our mother, in order to occupy my little sister while she sewed the doll clothes, let her "carefully" play with the doll while my sister and I were at school. This turned into the biggest joke all through our lives. Last year, I found reproductions of that same Barbie with the wig wardrobe. I purchased one for each of us. When Lisa received it, she called and we had the best time reminiscing and laughing about that childhood Christmas.

–Paula Anderson, Kingwood, TX

Caroling Party Supper

Mushroom Pizza

Jennifer Niemi
Nova Scotia, Canada

We almost never order take-out pizza at our house...I'd much rather have one of my own thick-crust pizzas, hot out of the oven and oh-so delicious!

1 to 2 t. olive oil
1 T. cornmeal
8-oz. can tomato sauce
1/2 t. sugar
1/4 t. pepper
3/4 t. garlic powder
1 T. dried marjoram

2 T. grated Parmesan cheese
1 c. onion, diced
3 10-oz. cans mushroom pieces, drained
1/2 lb. extra-sharp white Cheddar cheese, shredded

Prepare Pizza Dough. On a floured surface, roll out dough to a 15-inch by 10-inch rectangle. Transfer to a 15"x10" jelly-roll pan that has been greased generously with olive oil and sprinkled with cornmeal. In a bowl, combine tomato sauce, sugar and seasonings. Spread over crust. Top with remaining ingredients in order given. Bake at 400 degrees for 25 to 30 minutes, until crust edges turn golden. Serves 8.

Pizza Dough:

3 c. all-purpose flour, divided
1 env. quick-rising yeast
3/4 t. salt

2 T. olive oil
1 c. hot water

Mix together 2 cups flour, yeast and salt; set aside. Stir oil into hot water. Add to flour mixture; mix well. Stir in enough of remaining flour to make a soft dough. Knead on a lightly floured surface until dough is smooth and elastic, about 6 minutes. Cover; let stand for 10 minutes before rolling out.

An easy shortcut for Mushroom Pizza...buy a one-pound package of frozen or refrigerated pizza dough instead of making your own!

Tuscan Chicken Panini

Gail Blain Prather
Hastings, NE

It is no secret that I love my cast-iron cookware, and when I was given a grill pan as a gift, I set out to make the perfect panini sandwich. Of course, you could use a panini press to make this but I love the technique of using a cast-iron grill pan and a foil-wrapped brick. It works perfectly!

4 boneless, skinless chicken
    breasts
1/2 c. Italian salad dressing,
    divided
2 red peppers
8 slices hearty sourdough bread

4 slices smoked provolone
    cheese
8 fresh basil leaves
1 T. olive oil
Italian seasoning to taste

Marinate chicken breasts in 1/4 cup Italian dressing for at least 30 minutes. Meanwhile, heat a grill pan over medium-high heat and grill whole red peppers. Once the skin is blackened on all sides, place in a plastic zipping bag and allow to steam. Grill chicken breasts on grill pan on both sides until cooked through. Set aside. Remove skin and seeds from peppers; cut into strips. Brush each slice of bread with remaining Italian dressing. On 4 slices of bread, layer one chicken breast, 1/4 of red pepper strips, one slice of provolone cheese and 2 basil leaves; top with remaining bread slices. Brush outsides of sandwiches with olive oil; sprinkle with Italian seasoning. Place one sandwich at a time on the hot grill pan; press down with an aluminum foil-wrapped brick. Grill until bread is lightly toasted and cheese is melted. Turn and toast the other side. Repeat with remaining sandwiches. Makes 4 sandwiches.

Spend an evening baking homemade dog biscuits and cat treats...your friends will be touched when you remember their pets with a small treat!

Caroling Party Supper

Baked Nacho Sub

Nan Scarborough
Nacogdoches, TX

This beefy make-ahead sandwich is great for picnics or camping trips. It was my tradition to send one of these subs with my sons and their dad on their annual after-Christmas camping trip.

1 loaf French bread
1 lb. ground beef
1-1/4 pkg. taco seasoning mix
4-oz. can diced green chiles
10-3/4 oz. can nacho cheese
  soup
2 c. shredded Mexican-blend
  cheese, divided

Cut loaf in half lengthwise. Open up and hollow out halves, reserving bread pieces. In a skillet over medium heat, brown beef until no longer pink; drain. Add taco seasoning, chiles, reserved bread pieces and soup. Mix well and heat through. Stir in one cup cheese; spoon beef mixture into bottom half of bread loaf. Sprinkle with remaining cheese. Replace top half of loaf; wrap tightly in aluminum foil. Place on an ungreased baking sheet; bake at 350 degrees for 30 minutes, or until heated through. Slice to serve. Serves 6 to 8.

For a thoughtful gift that's easy on the wallet, purchase a calendar and fill in birthdays, anniversaries and other important family events...a nice gift for those new to the family!

Oven-Barbecued Chicken

Paula Eggleston
Knoxville, TN

When we have company over, this is a great recipe to double. There's always plenty. I serve this yummy chicken with yellow rice and spoon some extra sauce over both.

2 T. butter
1 onion, sliced
1/4 c. water
2 T. brown sugar, packed
1 T. Worcestershire sauce

1 c. catsup
1/4 t. garlic powder
1 t. salt
1/4 t. pepper
3 to 3-1/2 lbs. chicken

In a saucepan over medium heat, melt butter. Add onion; cook and stir until tender. Add remaining ingredients except chicken. Heat to boiling; reduce heat and simmer for 10 minutes, stirring occasionally. Arrange chicken pieces in an ungreased 13"x9" baking pan; spoon butter mixture over top. Bake, uncovered, at 350 degrees for one hour and 15 minutes, or until juices run clear when chicken is pierced. Serves 4.

Why not save the annual building of the gingerbread house until after Christmas? The kids are home on break, and you'll be able to enjoy the activity in a more relaxed fashion...and maybe even use up some leftover Christmas candy!

Caroling Party
Supper

Sour Cream Potato Cakes

JoAnn

These yummy little cakes are always a treat alongside any meal!

1 lb. Yukon gold potatoes,
   peeled
1-1/2 t. salt, divided
5 T. olive oil, divided
1/4 c. shredded Asiago cheese

5 T. sour cream
1/4 t. pepper
Garnish: sour cream, chopped
   fresh chives

Place potatoes and one teaspoon salt in a large saucepan; add enough water to cover. Cover; bring to a boil over medium-high heat. Uncover, reduce heat and boil potatoes until tender, about 20 to 25 minutes. Drain; mash potatoes until smooth. Return to saucepan. Add 3 tablespoons olive oil, cheese, sour cream and pepper. Divide mixture into quarters and shape each into a 3/4-inch thick patty. Heat remaining oil in a skillet over medium-high heat. Cook patties for 2 to 3 minutes, until a deep golden crust forms. Flip and cook other side 2 to 3 minutes. Garnish as desired. Makes 4 servings.

Making stacks of potato cakes for a crowd? Keep them warm
and yummy...just arrange cakes on a baking sheet,
set in a 200-degree oven, then serve as needed.

812 Bistro Spaghetti

Teresa Hall
Bristol, VA

Everyone loves spaghetti, and what can be better than homemade sauce? This recipe is named for my sister-in-law, and it's my go-to recipe every time I have to cook for a crowd. Everyone seems to come back for seconds, so I often double the recipe just to make sure there will be plenty.

16-oz. pkg. spaghetti, uncooked	2 t. garlic powder
1 lb. lean ground beef	2 T. Italian seasoning
1 onion, chopped	1 t. salt
1 green pepper, chopped	2 t. pepper
8-oz. can tomato sauce	1 c. shredded Cheddar cheese
6-oz. can tomato paste	1/2 c. grated Parmesan cheese
26-oz. jar spaghetti sauce	Garnish: additional grated
1 t. sugar	Parmesan cheese
2 T. dried oregano	

Prepare spaghetti according to package directions; drain. Meanwhile, in a deep skillet over medium heat, brown beef with onion and pepper; drain. Add remaining ingredients except cheeses. Cover skillet with lid; simmer over low heat for 45 minutes, stirring occasionally. Stir in cheeses. In a large serving bowl, combine spaghetti and sauce. Sprinkle with additional Parmesan cheese. Serves 10 to 12.

Give Frosty a pair of rosy cheeks! Mix five drops red food coloring with a cup of water; pour into a spray bottle. Finely mist your snowman's cheeks for just the right touch of color.

Caroling Party Supper

Sausage-Potato "Lasagna"

Sandra Sullivan
Aurora, CO

This recipe may seem complicated, but prep time is only about 35 minutes. You'll find it's worth the effort...yum!

1/2 lb. Italian ground pork
   sausage
2 c. sliced mushrooms
4 potatoes, peeled and thinly
   sliced
10-oz. pkg. frozen chopped
   spinach, thawed and drained
1-1/2 c. ricotta cheese
1/4 c. grated Parmesan cheese

1 egg, beaten
1 onion, chopped
2 cloves garlic, minced
2 T. butter
2 T. all-purpose flour
1/4 t. nutmeg
1-1/2 c. milk
1 c. shredded mozzarella cheese,
   divided

In a skillet over medium-high heat, brown sausage with mushrooms; drain and set aside. In a saucepan, cook potatoes in boiling water for 5 minutes; drain and set aside. In a bowl, stir together spinach, ricotta and Parmesan cheeses and egg; set aside. In a separate saucepan, cook onion and garlic in butter until onion is tender; stir in flour and nutmeg. Add milk. Cook and stir until mixture is thickened and bubbly; remove from heat. In a greased 2-quart rectangular casserole dish, layer half of the potatoes. Top with half each of the spinach mixture, sausage mixture, onion mixture and mozzarella cheese. Repeat layers, except for cheese. Cover with aluminum foil; bake at 350 degrees for 35 minutes, or until potatoes are tender. Uncover and sprinkle with remaining cheese; bake for an additional 5 minutes, or until cheese is melted. Let stand for 10 minutes before serving. Serves 6 to 8.

Wait until just before dinner to open the holiday cards that have arrived in that day's mail, so everyone gets to join in on the excitement!

Unstuffed Cabbage

Diane Cohen
The Woodlands, TX

Originally this recipe was for the stovetop, but I adapted it for the slow cooker. It's yummy served over mashed potatoes!

1 lb. ground beef
1/2 c. onion, chopped
1/2 c. celery, sliced
3 cloves garlic, finely chopped
1 head cabbage, chopped
28-oz. can stewed tomatoes
6-oz. can tomato paste
1 t. sugar

1-1/2 t. dried parsley
1 t. dried oregano
1/4 t. pepper
Optional: hot pepper sauce
   to taste
Garnish: shredded Cheddar
   cheese

In a large skillet over medium heat, cook beef, onion, celery and garlic until beef is no longer pink. Drain; transfer to a greased slow cooker. Top with cabbage. In a large bowl, combine tomatoes with juice and tomato paste. Break up tomatoes with a potato masher. Stir in sugar, seasonings and hot sauce, if using. Spoon over top of cabbage. Cover and cook on low setting for 8 to 10 hours. Top individual servings with shredded cheese. Serves 5 to 6.

Here's a fun no-sew craft for kids! Fill a clean white sock about 2/3 full with dry rice. Tie the sock closed about one inch above the rice. Divide the filled section of the sock almost in half to create a body and a head; tie tightly with a piece of yarn. Roll or fold down the top empty part of the sock so it looks like a hat. Now, use a variety of craft supplies to decorate your snowman... pompoms, googly eyes, buttons and felt are just a few ideas!

Caroling Party Supper

Sweet Glazed Meatloaf

Jennifer Carter
Hilliard, OH

My father-in-law loves meatloaf, but I could never find a recipe that I really enjoyed. So I started playing around with different ingredients one day and came up with this. My family goes crazy over it every time I make it!

3 lbs. ground beef
3 slices bread, toasted and
    coarsely crumbled
3 green onions, sliced
1 c. catsup, divided

2 eggs, beaten
1-1/2 T. Montreal steak
    seasoning
1/4 c. brown sugar, packed

In a large bowl, combine beef, toast crumbs, onions, 1/4 cup catsup, eggs and seasoning; mix well. Transfer to a 9"x5" loaf pan; bake at 375 degrees for one hour and 10 minutes. Remove from oven; drain off about 3/4 of the drippings. In a bowl, combine remaining catsup and brown sugar; spoon mixture over meatloaf. Return to the oven and bake for 10 to 15 minutes longer. Let stand 10 minutes before serving. Serves 8.

For a warm, cozy holiday fragrance, simmer cinnamon sticks, lemon or orange peel, whole cloves and nutmeg in a pot of water on the stovetop.

Angelic Scampi

Cyndy DeStefano
Mercer, PA

*We love shrimp scampi at our house, but we are trying to eat
healthier. So instead of giving it up, we tried making it better
for us...and to our surprise, the new version was better-tasting too!*

16-oz. pkg. angel hair pasta,
  uncooked
2 t. olive oil
4 cloves garlic, minced
1 t. dried oregano
1 lb. medium shrimp, peeled and
  cleaned

1/4 c. white cooking wine or
  chicken broth
2 t. cornstarch
3/4 c. chicken broth
salt and pepper to taste

Cook pasta according to package directions; drain and keep warm.
Meanwhile, heat oil in a large skillet over medium-high heat. Add
garlic; sauté one minute. Add oregano; stir to coat in oil. Add shrimp;
sauté until pink, about 3 minutes. Pour in 1/4 cup wine or broth;
reduce heat and simmer one minute. In a small bowl, dissolve
cornstarch in 3/4 cup chicken broth; add to skillet. Simmer about
2 minutes, until sauce thickens; season with salt and pepper. Transfer
cooked pasta to a large serving bowl; pour shrimp and sauce over top.
Toss before serving. Serves 4.

Quickly thaw frozen shrimp by placing the shrimp in
a colander and running cold water over them...they'll be
ready to cook in no time!

Caroling Party Supper

Francie's Greek Salad

Francie Stutzman
Clinton, OH

This simple salad is so good...I always take it to gatherings.

1 head iceberg lettuce, chopped
1 onion, diced
2 tomatoes, chopped

4-oz. pkg. crumbled feta cheese
1 c. pitted black olives

In a large serving bowl, combine all ingredients. Toss with Greek Dressing just before serving. Serves 8.

Greek Dressing:

1/3 c. canola oil
1/3 c. olive oil
1/3 c. red wine vinegar
1 T. dried oregano

2 t. salt
1 t. pepper
1 t. garlic powder

Combine all ingredients in a tightly covered jar; shake well.

Avoid soggy salads...simply pour salad dressing in
the bottom of your salad bowl, then add greens on top.
Toss just before serving.

Marilyn's Slow-Cooked Chicken & Noodles

Marilyn Stonecipher
Bloomington, IN

My family just loves this recipe, especially on a crisp evening after a nice day at the park. For me, it brings up memories of my childhood... although Momma made hers on the stovetop and made her own homemade dumplings instead of using noodles.

6 chicken thighs
salt and pepper to taste
3 stalks celery with leaves
4 carrots, peeled and chopped
2 cloves garlic, chopped

16-oz. can chicken broth
2 c. water
1 bay leaf
16-oz. pkg. wide egg noodles, uncooked

Add chicken to a slow cooker; sprinkle with salt and pepper. Add vegetables, broth, water and bay leaf. Cover and cook on high setting for 4 hours. Remove chicken and vegetables from slow cooker; discard celery stalks and bay leaf. Add noodles to liquid in slow cooker; cover and cook on high setting for 20 minutes, or until tender. Meanwhile, chop chicken, removing skin and bones. When noodles are tender, return chicken and carrots to slow cooker; heat through. Serves 8.

Make a snowman garland...it's easy! Use lengths of butcher paper and fold and cut as you would for a paper doll chain.

Caroling Party Supper

Delectable Baked Chicken

Jacquie Marquardt
Virgil, IL

This recipe was shared by a family friend years ago...it's a huge favorite in my family. Yummy!

8 boneless, skinless chicken
   breasts
2 c. sour cream
1/4 c. lemon juice
4 t. Worcestershire sauce
1 T. garlic salt
2 t. paprika

2 t. salt
2 t. pepper
1-1/2 to 2 c. dry bread crumbs
1/2 c. butter, melted
1/2 c. oil
cooked rice

Place chicken in a 13"x9" glass baking pan; set aside. In a bowl, combine sour cream, lemon juice, Worcestershire sauce and seasonings. Coat chicken evenly with sour cream mixture; cover and refrigerate overnight. About an hour before serving time, roll chicken in bread crumbs and return to pan. In a bowl, whisk together butter and oil; spoon half of mixture over chicken in pan. Bake, uncovered, at 350 degrees for 45 minutes. Spoon remaining butter mixture over chicken. Bake 15 minutes longer, just until chicken juices run clear when pierced. Serve with cooked rice. Makes 8 servings.

When I was six years old, my daddy was in Vietnam when Christmas rolled around. My mother, sister, brother and I all decided we were going to leave our Christmas tree up with all the gifts underneath and save Christmas for when Daddy got back. That was the best Christmas ever, about six months later!

–Debbie Schulte, Lenexa, KS

Cider-Marinated Ribs

Andrea Heyart
Aubrey, TX

As summer fades and cooler weather moves in, these ribs find themselves on our table on a weekly basis. Sweet and tender, they simply fall apart under a fork.

3 lbs. boneless country-style
   pork ribs
1-1/2 c. apple cider
1/2 c. orange juice
1 T. garlic, minced

1 T. Worcestershire sauce
salt and pepper
1 t. chili powder
1 c. barbecue sauce, divided

Place ribs in a large plastic zipping bag or a large pan with a lid. Add cider, orange juice, garlic and Worcestershire sauce. Seal; refrigerate for at least 3 hours, turning over once. Remove ribs from bag, discarding marinade; place in a 13"x9" glass baking pan. Season both sides generously with salt and pepper; sprinkle with chili powder. Baste with 1/2 cup barbecue sauce; cover with aluminum foil. Bake at 300 degrees for 2 hours. Remove foil; baste with remaining barbecue sauce. Bake, uncovered, for an additional 30 minutes. Serves 4.

Making salt dough ornaments is a fun holiday activity! Combine 2 cups flour, one cup water and one cup salt. Knead dough; roll out 1/2-inch thick. Use cookie cutters to cut into shapes; punch a hole for a hanger. Bake at 200 degrees for 15 minutes, or until hardened. Paint with craft paints; when dry, spray with acrylic sealer. Hang with baker's twine or yarn.

Caroling Party Supper

Coffee-Braised Beef Short Ribs

Gail Blain Prather
Hastings, NE

Cold weather always has me wanting to make a braised dish, and these short ribs are over-the-top good and comforting.

3 lbs. beef short ribs
salt and pepper to taste
2 T. olive oil, divided
1 yellow onion, chopped
3 cloves garlic, chopped

1-1/2 c. strong brewed coffee
2 T. balsamic vinegar
2 t. chili powder
1 t. dried oregano

Season ribs with salt and pepper. In a large Dutch oven over high heat, heat one tablespoon oil. Add ribs and cook, turning once, until browned, about 8 minutes. Transfer to a plate. Add remaining oil to Dutch oven; sauté onion and garlic until tender. Add coffee and vinegar. Cook and stir over high heat, scraping up brown bits from the bottom. Return ribs to Dutch oven; sprinkle with chili powder and oregano. Bake, covered, at 350 degrees for 1-1/2 hours, or until ribs are very tender. Serves 6.

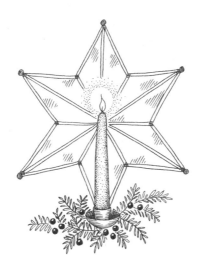

Looking for a tasty make-ahead dinner? Braised dishes gain a lot of flavor when allowed to rest for a day or two, so you can make them ahead of time, refrigerate and just reheat!

Tuna-Cheese Imperial

Paula Lopat
Warrenville, IL

This is not your ordinary tuna casserole and it's really easy to make! It's good comfort food on a chilly night. You can substitute two cups of cooked chicken or turkey for the tuna, if you wish.

8-oz. pkg. wide egg noodles, uncooked
1/2 c. margarine, divided
5 T. all-purpose flour
1 t. salt
1/4 t. pepper
2-1/2 c. milk
8-oz. pkg. cream cheese, cubed

2 6-oz. cans tuna, drained
2 T. fresh chives, chopped
Optional: 1/2 c. sliced black olives
8-oz. pkg. sliced Muenster cheese
1-1/2 c. soft bread crumbs

Cook noodles as directed on package; drain and set aside. Melt 5 tablespoons margarine in a medium saucepan; stir in flour, salt and pepper. Cook over medium heat, stirring constantly, until bubbly. Add milk; continue to cook and stir for 3 minutes, or until sauce thickens and bubbles. Add cream cheese; stir until melted. Add tuna, chives and olives, if using. Mix well; remove from heat. Pour one cup of tuna mixture into an ungreased 2-1/2 quart casserole dish. Layer with half the noodles, half the remaining tuna mixture and half the cheese slices. Repeat layers. Melt remaining margarine in a saucepan; add bread crumbs. Toss lightly with a fork just to moisten; sprinkle over top. Bake, uncovered, at 350 degrees for 30 minutes, or until bubbly. Serves 8.

Instead of hanging a treasured antique ornament from a hook, where it could be knocked down, secure it with a length of wire. Just thread wire through the hanging loop and wrap tightly around a branch.

Caroling Party Supper

Salmon Quiche

Marybeth Summers
Medford, OR

One of my mother's favorite uses for leftover salmon.

9-inch pie crust
8-oz. can salmon, drained
1/2 c. fresh parsley, chopped
1 c. shredded Swiss cheese
1/2 c. cream cheese, softened
2 t. fresh dill, chopped, or
    1/2 t. dill weed

1/2 c. whipping cream
3 eggs, beaten
1/4 t. salt
1/4 t. white pepper
1 T. lemon juice
paprika to taste

Place crust in a 9" pie plate. Pierce bottom of crust with a fork; bake at 425 degrees for 10 minutes. Allow to cool. Spoon salmon into crust; sprinkle with parsley and Swiss cheese. In a bowl, beat cream cheese, dill and cream until smooth. Add eggs, salt, pepper and lemon juice; beat until well combined. Spoon cream cheese mixture over Swiss cheese. Sprinkle with paprika. Bake at 350 degrees for 40 minutes. Allow to stand for 10 minutes before serving. Serves 6 to 8.

I remember as a young child heading to Grandma's house for Christmas Eve. All of my mom's brothers and sisters came with all of their children. As soon as we arrived, the cooking would begin. The cousins were sent outside to play, and the men built a big fire in the backyard. We would roast marshmallows and play games until we were too tired to play anymore. Grandma made us beds on the floor in the living room near the Christmas tree so we could wait for Santa...but we never made it that long. The mornings were full of fun and surprises, and lots of food! My grandma's brothers and sisters stopped by throughout the day with their families. At times there'd be 50 to 75 people scattered throughout the house and yard...what fun we had!

–Sophia Graves, Okeechobee, FL

Barbecups

Joanne Mauseth
Reno, NV

My daughter found this recipe when she was learning to cook.
Her dad requests these tasty little cups quite frequently.

1 lb. ground beef
1/4 c. onion, chopped
1/2 c. barbecue sauce

1 T. brown sugar, packed
12-oz. tube refrigerated biscuits
1/2 c. shredded Cheddar cheese

Grease 10 muffin cups. In a skillet over medium heat, brown beef
with onion; drain. Stir in barbecue sauce and sugar; cook one minute.
Separate biscuits; firmly press one into the bottom and up the sides of
each muffin cup. Spoon 1/4 cup beef mixture into each biscuit; sprinkle
with cheese. Bake at 400 degrees for 10 to 12 minutes, until biscuits
are golden. Cool; remove from tin. Makes 10.

Pick an evening for a family "card party." Whip up some
special snacks and spend the evening at the kitchen table
signing your Christmas cards. Keep one of your own signed
Christmas cards in a holiday scrapbook...it's a joy
to see the kids' signatures "grow up" over the years.

Classic Christmas
Dinner

Len's Poached Ham

Len Walker
Ontario, Canada

Enjoy the juiciest ham you will ever taste! I like to use a hickory-smoked ham but any good quality bone-in ham will work. This recipe is for a half ham. Just double the recipe for a whole ham.

10 to 12-lb. smoked ham
1 c. dark brown sugar, packed
2 8-oz. jars peach marmalade or
    jam
1 T. Dijon mustard
1/2 c. ginger marmalade

1/2 c. cider vinegar
1 T. honey
1-1/2 c. dry white wine
10 4-inch cinnamon sticks,
    broken in half
Garnish: green leaf lettuce

Place ham in a very large stockpot; cover with water. Over high heat, bring to a boil. Reduce heat; simmer, uncovered, for one hour. Combine remaining ingredients except wine, cinnamon sticks and garnish in a saucepan. Cook and stir over medium heat until a glaze forms; remove from heat and keep warm. Remove ham carefully from pot; transfer to a rack in a large roasting pan. Push cinnamon sticks into the ham, creating a "porcupine." Drizzle wine over ham first, then follow with glaze. Bake, uncovered, at 375 degrees for 45 minutes. Remove cinnamon sticks before slicing. To serve, arrange lettuce on a serving dish; place ham slices on top. Serve with pan drippings spooned over top. Serves 18 to 20.

Bake up a quiche with leftover ham, chopped veggies and cheese! Put about a cup of ingredients in a pie crust, then whisk together 3 eggs and a small can of evaporated milk. Pour into crust and bake at 400 degrees until set, about 20 to 25 minutes. Scrumptious any time of day!

Classic Christmas Dinner

Holiday Ham Glaze

Peggy Donnally
Toledo, OH

I created this glaze after many years of experimenting. Everyone loved it! So now every holiday, I make sure that I have all the ingredients on hand for our family's new "traditional" glaze.

1 c. mango chutney
1/4 c. Dijon mustard
1 c. dark brown sugar, packed
1/4 t. ground cloves
zest of 1 orange
juice of 2 oranges

In a bowl, combine all ingredients. Spread over ham before baking. Makes enough to coat one ham.

When I was a child, my dad made the excitement of Christmas into a guessing game for my two older sisters and me. He said if we could figure out this puzzle we would know what one of our gifts would be. "It's round as a biscuit, busy as a bee, and it's the prettiest little thing you ever did see," he said. Of course, with the imaginations of seven, nine and ten-year-olds, we guessed everything imaginable, except the answer, which was a watch! We each received a new watch...mine was a Woody Woodpecker. That is one of my favorite Christmas memories.

–Pam Massey, Marshall, AR

Roast Turkey Breast

Kimberly Marlatt
Yuma, AZ

Last year, I used an electric roaster to cook our Christmas turkey...the results were wonderful! Not only did it cook much faster, but it was also moist, delicious and beautifully golden.

8-1/2 lb. turkey breast, thawed
1/2 c. butter, softened
2 to 3 cloves garlic, minced
1 to 1-1/2 t. poultry seasoning

1/8 t. pepper
1 lemon, halved
1 orange, halved
3 c. turkey or chicken broth

Remove gravy packet and giblets from turkey, if necessary, and discard. Pat turkey dry with paper towels. In a bowl, combine butter, garlic and seasonings. Add one tablespoon juice from lemon; mix well. Using your hands, loosen turkey skin from breast. Spread a few tablespoons of butter mixture under the skin and over the meat. Once you take your hands out, you can "massage" the skin to help spread the butter mixture around underneath. Spread 2 more tablespoons of butter mixture over the outer skin. Place orange and lemon halves inside the cavity. Pour broth into a roasting pan, under the rack. Place prepared turkey on the rack; cover with aluminum foil. Bake at 350 degrees for one hour. Remove foil; using a basting brush, brush remaining butter mixture over turkey. Cover; bake for one more hour, or until turkey is fully cooked and a meat thermometer reads 165 to 170 degrees when inserted into breast. Remove from roaster and let stand, covered with foil, for about 15 to 20 minutes before slicing. Serves 6 to 8.

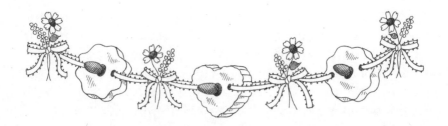

String together some old-fashioned cookie cutters with a cheery ribbon and add your own embellishments...what a festive addition to your Christmas kitchen!

Classic Christmas
❧ **Dinner** ❧

Nutcracker Potato Bake

Ashley Trask
Kentville, NS

This is a recipe that my family has been making every Christmas Eve for years when we all gather together. It's a favorite among family and guests, and one of the simplest recipes I've ever made.

10-3/4 oz. can cream of
   mushroom soup
8-oz. container sour cream
1/4 c. butter, softened
1 onion, chopped
2 c. shredded Cheddar cheese,
   divided

32-oz. pkg. frozen shredded
   potatoes
salt and pepper to taste
1 to 2 c. sour cream & onion
   potato chips, crushed

In a large bowl, combine soup, sour cream, butter, onion and one cup cheese. Stir in potatoes. Blend well; mixture will be thick. Press into a greased 12"x8" baking pan. Sprinkle with salt, pepper, remaining cheese and chips. Bake, uncovered, at 350 degrees for 45 minutes to one hour, until bubbly and golden. Serves 10 to 12.

Homemade pan gravy is delicious and easy to make. After removing the turkey to a platter, set the roaster with pan juices on the stovetop over medium heat. Shake together 1/4 cup cold water and 1/4 cup cornstarch in a small jar; pour into the roaster. Cook and stir until gravy comes to a boil and thickens, about 5 to 10 minutes. Add salt and pepper to taste, and it's ready to serve.

Easy-Made Braciole

Madonna Alexander
Chicago, IL

I make this Italian dish (pronounced bree-zshole) every Christmas Eve. It has become our official dish for the holidays. I serve it with penne or rigatoni pasta, hot crusty bread and a green salad.

1 lb. beef sandwich steaks or very thinly sliced beef round steak or sirloin
3 cloves garlic, minced
1/2 c. dry bread crumbs
1/4 c. fresh flat-leaf parsley, chopped
1/2 c. shredded Parmesan cheese
salt and pepper to taste
26-oz. jar favorite-flavor spaghetti sauce

Sprinkle each steak with about 1/8 teaspoon garlic, one teaspoon bread crumbs, 1/2 teaspoon parsley, one teaspoon Parmesan cheese, salt and pepper. Roll steaks up tightly; tie in 3 places with kitchen string or secure with 2 to 3 wooden toothpicks. Pour half of sauce into an ungreased 13"x9" baking pan. Arrange steak rolls over top. Pour remaining sauce over rolls; sprinkle with remaining Parmesan cheese. Cover pan with aluminum foil; bake at 325 degrees for 2 to 3 hours, until steaks are fork-tender. Makes 4 to 6 servings.

Classic Christmas ~❦~ **Dinner** ~❦~

Lasagna Rolls

Laura Hack
Sugar Creek, WY

These festive rolls can be served as a main dish or an appetizer.

1 lb. Italian ground pork
   sausage
1 onion, chopped
3 cloves garlic, pressed
3 T. olive oil
28-oz. can crushed tomatoes
Italian seasoning to taste

16-oz. pkg. lasagna noodles,
   uncooked
1 to 2 c. ricotta cheese
16-oz. pkg. shredded Italian-
   blend cheese
1 c. shredded Parmesan cheese
1 c. shredded mozzarella cheese

In a skillet over medium heat, brown sausage, onion and garlic in oil; drain. Crumble sausage. Add tomatoes and seasoning; simmer over low heat. Meanwhile, cook lasagna noodles as directed on package; drain and lay out on a clean tea towel. On each noodle, spread a thin layer of ricotta cheese, sprinkle some Italian-blend cheese and spoon a layer of sausage mixture down the center. Roll up noodle jelly-roll style and secure with a wooden toothpick. Spread a thin layer of sausage mixture in an ungreased 13"x9" baking pan. Place rolls, seam-side down, in pan; cover with remaining sausage mixture. Sprinkle with Parmesan and mozzarella cheeses. Cover with aluminum foil; bake at 350 degrees for 45 minutes, or until heated through and bubbly. Remove foil for the last 10 minutes of baking time. Serves 5.

Turn a toboggan into a clever wintertime serving table!
Just set it securely on top of a buffet table, toss on a plaid throw
and then load it up with lots of salads, sides and breads.

Frosty Waldorf Salad

Susan Bick
Ballwin, MO

A fruity favorite at all of our family gatherings.

1/2 c. sugar
1/2 c. pineapple juice
1/4 c. lemon juice
1/8 t. salt
1/4 c. celery, diced
1/2 c. mini marshmallows
1/2 c. seedless red grapes, halved

1/4 c. diced pears, drained
1/2 c. crushed pineapple, drained
2 apples, cored and diced
1/4 c. chopped walnuts
1/4 c. chopped pecans
1-1/3 c. whipping cream

Combine sugar, juices and salt in a large saucepan. Cook over medium heat, stirring often, until thickened. Remove from heat; let cool completely. Stir in celery, marshmallows, fruit and nuts. In a chilled bowl with an electric mixer on medium speed, whip cream until soft peaks form; fold into fruit mixture. Spoon into an ungreased 8"x8" baking pan; freeze. Remove from freezer 5 minutes before serving. Cut into squares to serve. Serves 9.

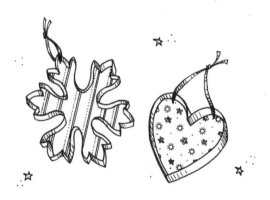

Use thrift-store cookie cutters to make a baker's dozen of adorable kitchen decorations! Choose thick scrapbook paper or color-copy photos onto cardstock. Trace cutter shape on top; cut out paper shape. Dab craft glue along the cutter's edge. Press paper in place; let dry. Attach hangers by threading a narrow ribbon through a needle.

Classic Christmas
❦ Dinner ☙

Christmas Celebration Salad
Cyndy DeStefano
Mercer, PA

New to our holiday menu last year, this salad has quickly become a favorite. The cranberries add that festive flavor and colorful touch...perfect for the Christmas table.

1 t. salt
2 apples, peeled, cored and
  chopped
4 c. mixed salad greens
1/2 c. sweetened dried
  cranberries

1/2 c. glazed almonds
1/2 c. crumbled blue cheese or
  Gorgonzola cheese

Dissolve salt in a medium bowl of warm water; add apples to water and let stand several minutes. In a serving bowl, combine remaining ingredients. Drain apples; add to salad. Drizzle Celebration Dressing over top; toss before serving. Serves 4.

Celebration Dressing:

1/3 c. cider vinegar
1/3 c. honey
1 t. cinnamon

1/2 t. salt
1/4 c. olive oil

In a small bowl, whisk together all ingredients except oil. Add oil in a slow stream, whisking constantly, until mixture is smooth. Dressing may be prepared up to 2 weeks ahead of time and stored in the refrigerator in an airtight container.

Think of a few questions to ask during Christmas dinner. What's a favorite holiday memory? What's your Christmas wish this year? What about a New Year's goal? It's a nice way to share sweet memories and catch up with family & friends during this special time of year.

Incredible Baked Cabbage
Kelly Serdynski Gray
Weston, WV

This is my cousin Keightley's baked cabbage. It's a real hit at our annual Christmas Eve gathering. Keightley is the "glue" that holds our family together. She is one of the last of the wild Stursa women who ran one of the first beauty parlors in Bartow, Florida. These ladies knew how to live! Cousin Keightley and Cousin Jen, her daughter-in-law, now are part of the Bartow, Florida Citrus Queens. They just up and have a parade whenever they decide it is time to party...and they always have lots of food to share.

3 c. cabbage, shredded
1/4 c. mayonnaise
1 t. mustard
1 T. chopped pimento
2 eggs
1-1/3 c. milk

salt and pepper to taste
6 slices bread, buttered and
   cubed
1 c. shredded Monterey Jack or
   Pepper Jack cheese
1 c. shredded Swiss cheese

In a saucepan, cover cabbage with water. Bring to a boil over high heat. Cook until tender; drain. Add mayonnaise, mustard and pimento. In a bowl, whisk together eggs, milk, salt and pepper. In a greased 2-quart casserole dish, stir together cabbage mixture, bread cubes and cheeses; pour egg mixture over top, blending well. Bake, uncovered, at 350 degrees for 30 minutes. Serves 8 to 12.

For a simple yet impressive table decoration, spray paint tree branches and twigs snow white or gleaming silver. Allow to dry, then brush with craft glue and sprinkle with glitter. Arrange the twigs in a tall vase...you can even hang some mini ornaments from the branches!

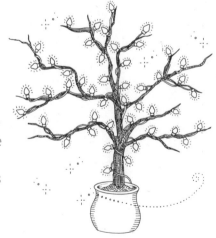

Classic Christmas
❧ Dinner ❧

Hot Bacon Brussels Sprouts
Ann Mathis
Biscoe, AR

*Even if your guests say they don't like Brussels sprouts,
they will love these...they are awesome!*

3 lbs. Brussels sprouts,
    quartered
2 T. olive oil
1 t. salt

10 slices bacon, chopped
1/2 c. balsamic vinegar
2 T. brown sugar, packed
1 t. Dijon mustard

In a large bowl, toss Brussels sprouts with olive oil and salt. Place on
a rimmed baking sheet lined with aluminum foil. Bake at 400 degrees
for 20 minutes, or until tender. In a large skillet over medium-high heat,
cook bacon until crisp. Using a slotted spoon, remove bacon; drain on
paper towels. Reserve 1/4 cup drippings in skillet. Add remaining
ingredients to skillet. Cook over medium-high heat, stirring frequently,
for 6 minutes, or until mixture is reduced by half. Drizzle over sprouts,
tossing gently to coat. Sprinkle with bacon. Serves 10 to 12.

Red & Green Potato Salad
Marilyn Westendorf
Tampa, FL

My husband and I served this tasty salad at our wedding reception.

2-1/2 lbs. redskin potatoes,
    cubed
1 lb. green beans, trimmed and
    cut into 2-inch pieces
salt to taste
1 c. creamy Caesar salad
    dressing

1/2 c. shredded Parmesan
    cheese
1 t. garlic pepper
Garnish: additional shredded
    Parmesan cheese

Place potatoes and beans in a large stockpot; cover with water and add
salt. Cook over medium heat for about 20 minutes, or until tender.
Drain; allow to cool. In a large serving bowl, mix salad dressing,
cheese and garlic pepper. Add potatoes and beans; stir gently until well
combined. Garnish with additional Parmesan cheese. Serves 8 to 10.

Mom's Perfect Prime Rib

Carol Sue Bullick
Royersford, PA

My oldest son Michael always requests this for his birthday dinner.
He says he can't get a better prime rib dinner than this anywhere!

5-lb. beef rib roast
1/4 to 1/2 c. balsamic vinegar
2 T. garlic, minced
2 T. fresh thyme, chopped,
　or 2 t. dried thyme

1 T. fresh rosemary, chopped,
　or 1 t. dried rosemary
2 T. salt
1 T. olive oil

Place roast fat-side up in a shallow roasting pan. Brush entire surface with balsamic vinegar. In a small bowl, combine remaining ingredients. Coat top, sides and ends of beef with garlic mixture. Bake, uncovered, at 450 degrees for 15 minutes. Reduce heat to 325 degrees. Bake for 20 minutes longer per pound, or until a meat thermometer reads 145 degrees for rare or 160 degrees for medium. Remove from oven; tent with aluminum foil and let stand for 10 to 15 minutes. Slice; serve with pan drippings. Serves 6.

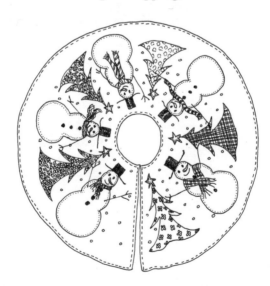

In need of a tree skirt? A jolly vintage Christmas tablecloth with its brightly colored images of Santas, elves or carolers is easily wrapped around the tree for a bit of old-fashioned holiday fun.

Classic Christmas
❧ Dinner ☙

Caroline's Oyster Casserole

Sherry Hallfors
Las Vegas, NV

My grandmother Caroline made this dish every Thanksgiving and Christmas...now, so do I.

4 to 5 sleeves saltine crackers,
    coarsely crushed
2 pts. oysters, drained and
    chopped

1 lb. butter, sliced
4 c. milk

Arrange some of the crushed crackers in a single layer in a greased 2-1/2 quart round casserole dish. Arrange a layer of oysters and several butter slices over top. Continue layering, finishing with crushed crackers topped with several butter slices. Slowly pour milk into the dish, just until it covers the top layer. Cover with aluminum foil; bake at 375 degrees for 35 minutes. Remove foil and bake 15 minutes longer, until golden and bubbly. Serves 10.

A thrifty way to make your own bread crumbs! Spread leftover bread heels with butter and freeze in a plastic zipping bag. When the bag is full, tear bread into pieces, place on a large baking sheet and place in a very low oven for several hours to dry out completely. After drying, place bread pieces in a food processor about 2 cups at a time. Process until finely chopped. Freeze for future use.

Spinach Noodle Kugel

Gina McClenning
Nicholson, GA

We make this kugel for all major holidays at our home. It's even better the next day! It's a nice accompaniment to meat dishes.

1 onion, chopped
1/2 c. butter, divided
3 cloves garlic, pressed
16-oz. pkg. fine or medium egg
    noodles, uncooked
2 9-oz. pkgs. frozen creamed
    spinach

16-oz. container sour cream
2 eggs, beaten
1 t. nutmeg
salt and pepper to taste
3/4 c. dry bread crumbs
1/2 c. grated Parmesan cheese

In a skillet over medium heat, sauté onion in 1/4 cup butter until tender. Add garlic; cook and stir for 2 more minutes. Remove from heat; set aside. Cook noodles according to package directions. Drain; transfer to a large bowl. Toss noodles with remaining butter. Cook creamed spinach according to package directions. Add spinach to noodles; stir in sour cream, onion mixture, eggs and seasonings. Pour into a buttered 3-quart casserole dish; sprinkle with bread crumbs and Parmesan cheese. Bake, uncovered, at 350 degrees for 45 minutes to one hour. Serves 6 to 8.

Many merry Christmases, friendships, great accumulation
of cheerful recollections, affection on earth...
heaven at last for all of us.

–Charles Dickens

Classic Christmas
❧ Dinner ☙

Filsel (Pennsylvania Dutch Potatoes)

Rebecca Ludman
Hellertown, PA

My step-grandmother would make this recipe every Christmas Eve.
It is so delicious and a definite comfort food.

4 baking potatoes, peeled and
   cubed
1 onion, chopped
3 T. celery with leaves, chopped
1/4 c. butter, divided
3 slices bread, cubed

3 T. fresh parsley, chopped
1/2 t. salt
pepper to taste
1 c. milk, warmed
1 egg, beaten

In a large saucepan, cover potatoes with water. Bring to a boil; cook over high heat until fork-tender. Drain; mash potatoes and set aside. In a skillet over medium heat, sauté onion and celery in 2 tablespoons butter. When onion turns golden, add bread. Cook and stir until bread cubes are toasted. Add onion mixture, parsley, salt and pepper to mashed potatoes. Add warm milk gradually. Beat with an electric mixer on medium speed until well blended. Add egg; beat until well blended. Transfer to a greased 8"x8" baking pan. Dot with remaining butter. Bake, uncovered, at 350 degrees for 30 minutes, or until heated through. Serves 6.

Paperwhite narcissus bulbs are easy to plant, and fast growing too! Plant in pots four to six weeks before Christmas and you'll enjoy their tiny white flowers on your holiday table.

Merry Sweet Potatoes

Michelle Papp
Rutherford, NJ

This side is a favorite holiday dish in my family.

6 sweet potatoes
3 T. butter, melted
2 T. orange juice
1/2 t. vanilla extract
1 t. cinnamon
1/2 t. nutmeg

salt and pepper to taste
3/4 c. sweetened dried
  cranberries
1/2 c. brown sugar, packed
1/2 c. chopped pecans

Wrap sweet potatoes individually in aluminum foil; place on a baking sheet. Bake at 350 degrees for one hour. Allow to cool. Cut each sweet potato in half; scoop out the insides into a large bowl. Discard skins. Add butter, orange juice, vanilla, cinnamon, nutmeg, salt and pepper; stir until smooth. Fold in cranberries. Pour into an 8"x8" baking pan that has been coated with non-stick vegetable spray. Smooth top with a spoon. Sprinkle brown sugar and pecans over top. Bake, uncovered, at 350 degrees for 15 minutes, or until warmed through. Serves 6.

Toss some candied nuts over a salad or side dish for a special touch. To make, whisk one egg white with one teaspoon cold water and toss a pound of shelled nuts in this mixture. Mix one cup sugar, one teaspoon cinnamon and 1/2 teaspoon salt; coat the nuts well. Spread nuts on a greased baking sheet. Bake at 225 degrees for one hour, stirring once or twice. Store in an airtight container.

Classic Christmas
❧ Dinner ☙

Festive Stuffed Acorn Squash
Gladys Kielar
Perrysburg, OH

*Every day feels like a holiday when you serve
these festive fruit-filled squash!*

2 acorn squash
1/4 t. salt
2 c. tart apples, cored and
   chopped
3/4 c. fresh or frozen cranberries

1/4 c. brown sugar, packed
2 T. butter, melted
1/4 t. cinnamon
1/8 t. nutmeg

Cut squash in half; remove seeds. Place squash cut-side down in an
ungreased baking pan. Add one inch hot water to the pan. Bake,
uncovered, at 350 degrees for 30 minutes. Drain water. Turn squash
cut-side up; sprinkle with salt. In a bowl, combine remaining
ingredients; spoon into squash. Bake, uncovered, 50 minutes longer,
or until squash is tender. Serves 4.

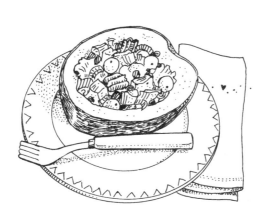

Need extra oven space? Try roasting veggies in the slow cooker.
You won't even need to add any water or oil! The vegetables
have enough of their own water to cook properly.

123

Elegant Cranberry Chutney

Pat Martin
Riverside, CA

I never really cared for cranberries until I found this chutney recipe. It's sweet, crunchy and a beautiful deep red color. It makes a wonderful side dish or topping for turkey or chicken. I can just eat it with a spoon!

16-oz. pkg. fresh cranberries
2 c. sugar
1 c. water
1 c. orange juice
1 c. chopped walnuts

1 c. celery, diced
1 apple, cored and chopped
1 T. orange zest
1 t. ground ginger

In a deep saucepan or Dutch oven over medium heat, bring cranberries, sugar and water to a boil, stirring frequently. Reduce heat to low; simmer 15 minutes. Remove from heat; stir in remaining ingredients. Refrigerate for up to a week in an airtight container. Makes 7 cups.

A quick-as-a-wink table runner...lay wide ribbon across the table's length and width.

Classic Christmas
❧ Dinner ☙

Rosemary Roasted Turkey

Zoe Bennett
Columbia, SC

What could be better than the aroma of turkey roasting in the oven?

3/4 c. olive oil
3 T. garlic, minced
2 T. fresh rosemary, chopped
1 T. dried basil

1 T. Italian seasoning
1 t. pepper
salt to taste
12-lb. turkey

In a small bowl, combine all ingredients except turkey. Set aside. Using your hands, loosen turkey skin from breast. Work skin loose to the end of the drumstick, being careful not to tear skin. Rub a generous amount of olive oil mixture under skin. Rub remaining mixture over the outside of skin. Use wooden toothpicks to fasten skin over any exposed meat. Place turkey on the rack in a roasting pan; add about 1/4 inch water to bottom of pan. Bake, uncovered, at 325 degrees for 3 to 4 hours, until temperature on a meat thermometer reads 165 degrees when inserted into the breast. Let stand 20 to 30 minutes before carving. Makes 16 servings.

For the freshest flavor, buy spices in small amounts, as they are perishable. Some specialty stores and markets offer spices in bulk containers so you can purchase the exact amount you need.

Grandma's Chestnut Stuffing
Nikki Matusiak
Zelienople, PA

When I was growing up, my family enjoyed this unusual stuffing every Thanksgiving. This recipe has been passed down from my grandmother, Mary Floros, who came to the United States from Greece in 1925. She used to get up at 5 a.m. to prepare our turkey and stuffing. These days, we bake the stuffing separately to cut down on turkey cooking time.

3 lbs. ground beef, browned and
    drained
1 c. cooked rice
40 to 50 chestnuts, roasted,
    peeled and coarsely ground
3 eggs, beaten

1/2 c. dry bread crumbs
1/4 c. cracker meal
1/2 to 1 c. onion, chopped
salt and pepper to taste
14-1/2 oz. can turkey or chicken
    broth

In a large bowl, combine all ingredients. Press mixture into a lightly greased 13"x9" baking pan. Bake, covered, at 350 degrees for one hour. May also be used to stuff a 10 to 12-pound turkey before roasting; do not add broth. Serves 8 to 10.

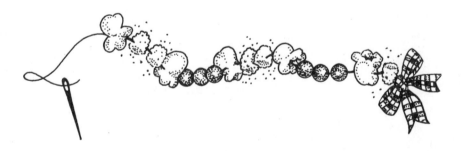

Making popcorn garlands to decorate the house? After popping the corn, set it aside for a couple of days. Stale popcorn is easier to string.

Classic Christmas ## ❦ **Dinner** ❧

Salmon Pie with Cream Sauce *Wendy Carlson*
Eugene, OR

Salmon was a childhood favorite. Mom used to make a salmon loaf with a cream egg sauce, but our family likes this pie even better!

1 onion, chopped
2 14-3/4 oz. cans salmon,
   drained
2 c. round buttery crackers,
   crushed

3/4 c. evaporated milk
1 T. coarse pepper
2 eggs, beaten
2 c. shredded Cheddar cheese
1 T. fresh parsley, chopped

In a lightly greased skillet over medium heat, sauté onion until tender. Combine onion and remaining ingredients in a greased 9" pie plate. Bake at 350 degrees for 35 minutes, or until set in the center. Allow to cool slightly; cut into wedges. Serve with White Wine Cream Sauce. Serves 6.

White Wine Cream Sauce:

1/2 c. dry white wine or chicken
   broth
1/4 c. lemon juice
1 T. sugar

1 t. salt
1 T. coarse pepper
1/8 t. dried thyme
1 c. whipping cream

In a medium saucepan, combine wine or broth, lemon juice, sugar and seasonings. Bring to a boil, stirring occasionally, until reduced by half. Reduce heat to medium; add cream. Cook, stirring often, until mixture thickens.

Recycle your Christmas tree! Remove the branches with a handsaw, and layer them over tender perennials in a crisscross pattern to protect the plants from the cold.

Winter Squash Risotto

Crystalyn Nield
Chatsworth, CA

A really big time-saver for a busy cook is to purchase the butternut squash already chopped...look in the grocery's produce section. You can also substitute pumpkin or any other type of squash you like.

2 lbs. butternut squash, peeled
   and chopped
2 T. olive oil
1 t. salt, divided
1 t. pepper, divided
3-1/2 c. chicken broth
1/4 c. butter, divided
1/8 lb. pancetta or bacon, finely
   chopped

1 clove garlic, minced
1 c. Arborio rice, uncooked
1/2 c. dry white wine or chicken
   broth
1 t. saffron or 1/8 t. turmeric
3/4 c. grated Parmesan cheese

In a bowl, combine squash, oil, 1/2 teaspoon salt and 1/2 teaspoon pepper. Toss to coat squash. Arrange squash in a single layer on a rimmed baking sheet. Bake at 400 degrees for 20 to 25 minutes, stirring halfway through. Meanwhile, in a saucepan over medium heat, bring broth to a simmer; reduce heat to low and keep warm. In a large skillet over medium heat, melt 2 tablespoons butter; sauté pancetta or bacon until golden. Add garlic; cook until tender. Add uncooked rice; stir to coat. Add wine or extra broth; sauté rice for 2 minutes, or until liquid is absorbed. Slowly add one cup warmed broth to skillet, stirring frequently; add saffron or turmeric and remaining salt. Cook until broth is mostly absorbed and rice begins to get creamy. Continue adding broth, one ladle at a time, stirring occasionally, until broth is used up and rice is tender, about 30 minutes. Stir in remaining pepper and butter. Fold in squash; sprinkle with Parmesan cheese. Serve immediately. Serves 4.

Wreaths aren't just for hanging!
Laid flat, one also can serve
as a base for a centerpiece or
a punch bowl on the buffet table.

Classic Christmas
❧ Dinner ❧

Roasted Pork Tenderloins

Sue Klapper
Muskego, WI

I love to make this recipe when I have company.
The pork is so tender and flavorful.

2 T. olive oil
2 T. cider vinegar
1 T. Dijon mustard
1 t. dried rosemary
1 t. dried thyme
1/2 t. garlic powder
1/2 t. salt
1/2 t. pepper

2 1-1/2 lb. pork tenderloins
6 to 8 potatoes, peeled and cut
 into wedges
4 to 6 carrots, peeled and cut
 into chunks
1 to 2 red peppers, cut into
 chunks
1 to 2 onions, cut into wedges

In a small bowl, combine oil, vinegar, mustard and seasonings; mix well. Place tenderloins in a shallow roasting pan; brush half the oil mixture evenly over both sides of each pork tenderloin. In a large bowl, toss remaining oil mixture with vegetables. Place vegetables alongside pork tenderloins. Bake, uncovered, at 425 degrees for 35 to 45 minutes, or until a meat thermometer inserted into the center of tenderloins reads 160 degrees. Serves 8.

For a sparkly centerpiece in a jiffy, arrange shiny vintage
balls in a glass trifle bowl. As easy as it gets!

Wild Rice & Pecan Stuffing

Leah Dodson
Covington, KY

I made this last year for Thanksgiving and it was a hit! The next morning we were making omelets and, being silly, we added in some of this stuffing. They were amazing!

7 c. chicken broth, divided
1-1/2 c. long-grain and wild rice
　mix, uncooked
1-1/2 c. long-cooking rice,
　uncooked
1/2 c. butter
2 onions, chopped
1-1/2 c. celery, chopped
1 c. sliced mushrooms
2 cloves garlic, minced
1 t. poultry seasoning
1/2 t. pepper
salt to taste
1/4 c. white wine or chicken
　broth
2 eggs, beaten
1 c. chopped pecans
1/4 c. fresh parsley, chopped

In a large saucepan over high heat, bring 6-1/2 cups broth to a boil; add all the rice. Reduce heat; cover and simmer 30 minutes, until rice is tender and broth is absorbed. Transfer to a large bowl. In a large skillet over medium heat, melt butter. Add onions and celery; sauté for 10 minutes. Add mushrooms, garlic and seasonings; cook until vegetables are tender, about 8 to 10 minutes. Add wine or broth; bring to a boil. Pour butter mixture over rice. Stir in eggs, remaining broth, pecans and parsley. Press into a greased 13"x9" baking pan. Bake, covered, at 350 degrees for 30 minutes. May also be used to stuff a 10 to 12-pound turkey. Serves 12 to 15.

Tied with a bright red bow, a galvanized pail is just right for filling with sand and fat pillar candles. Line up a few along your porch steps for a festive welcome.

Classic Christmas
❧ Dinner ☙

Escalloped Carrots

Ronda Smith
Mason City, IA

My great-aunt first introduced this recipe to our family. It quickly became a "must" at every family event!

10 carrots, peeled, cooked
   and mashed
1 onion, chopped
2 eggs, beaten
1 c. milk
3/4 t. salt

1/2 t. sugar
1/2 c. saltine crackers, crushed
3 T. butter, melted
1/4 c. shredded Cheddar cheese
Optional: additional sliced butter

In a large bowl, combine carrots, onion, eggs, milk, salt and sugar. In a separate bowl, toss crushed crackers with butter. In a lightly greased 1-1/2 quart casserole dish, spread half the carrot mixture; sprinkle with half the cheese and half the cracker mixture. Repeat layers. If desired, dot with additional butter before baking. Bake, uncovered, at 325 degrees for 30 to 35 minutes. Serves 10.

No fireplace? Hang stockings from stair railings, doorknobs, bookshelves or the backs of chairs!

Twice-Baked Sweet Potatoes
Gina McClenning
Nicholson, GA

*I can't resist sweet potatoes when they're in season...this is a
delicious dish that goes well with chicken, beef or pork!*

2 sweet potatoes
1 T. brown sugar, packed
2 T. butter, softened
1/2 t. orange zest

1/8 t. nutmeg
1/2 t. cinnamon
1/3 c. sweetened dried
   cranberries

Pierce sweet potatoes with a fork; bake at 350 degrees for 55 to
65 minutes, until tender. Slice potatoes in half; scoop out the insides
and place potato skins on a baking sheet. In a bowl, mix mashed
potatoes, sugar, butter, zest and spices; beat well. Fold in cranberries.
Fill potato skins with mixture. Bake for an additional 20 to 25 minutes,
until heated through. Serves 2 to 4.

Parsnip & Pear Purée
Joyceann Dreibelbis
Wooster, OH

*An unusual side dish, this sweet-tasting and easy-to-make
purée goes well with any kind of roast.*

2 lbs. parsnips, peeled and sliced
1 lb. ripe pears, peeled, cored
   and quartered

5 T. sour cream
salt and pepper to taste

In a large saucepan over medium-high heat, cover parsnips with
water and cook until tender, about 25 minutes. Add pears; cook for
5 minutes longer, or until tender. Drain. Purée parsnips and pears with
a food processor or a blender; stir in sour cream, salt and pepper. Serve
immediately or transfer to a casserole dish and reheat at serving time.
Serves 6 to 8.

Root vegetables like potatoes, carrots and onions grow tender
and sweet with all-day slow cooking. Give sweet potatoes
and parsnips a try too...delicious!

Classic Christmas
❧ Dinner ☙

Stuffed Turkey Roulade

Kathy Kexel
Marshfield, WI

I created this recipe for Thanksgiving dinner one year when it was just my mother, my brother and me. It was delicious...a delightful change from a whole turkey.

10 slices thick-cut bacon,
   divided
1/2 c. onion, chopped
2 cloves garlic, minced
8-oz. pkg. sliced mushrooms
1 c. ricotta cheese
3/4 c. shredded Swiss cheese
1/2 c. dry bread crumbs
2 eggs, beaten
1/4 t. nutmeg

1 t. salt, divided
2 10-oz. pkgs. frozen chopped
   spinach, thawed and drained
15-oz. jar marinated artichoke
   hearts, drained and chopped
4 to 6-lb. boneless turkey
   breast, butterflied
1-1/2 t. turkey rub, divided
2 T. olive oil or butter, melted

In a skillet over medium heat, cook 5 slices bacon until crisp. Crumble and set aside, reserving drippings in skillet. Sauté onion and garlic in drippings until soft. Add mushrooms; cook until edges begin to turn golden. Remove from heat; cool. In a bowl, combine cheeses, bread crumbs, eggs, nutmeg and 1/2 teaspoon salt; stir in spinach and artichokes. Add onion mixture to cheese mixture; blend well and set aside. Lay turkey flat, skin-side up. Season with 1/4 teaspoon salt and one teaspoon turkey rub. Turn turkey over. Season with remaining salt and turkey rub; spread with cheese mixture to within one inch of edges. Roll up jelly-roll style; tie with kitchen string. Place turkey skin-side up on a rack in a greased roasting pan; rub with oil or butter. Cover loosely with aluminum foil. Bake at 350 degrees for one hour. Halve remaining bacon slices; arrange over turkey basket-weave style. Bake, uncovered, for an additional 25 to 35 minutes, until a meat thermometer inserted in thickest part reads 165 degrees. Cover again with foil; let stand 15 minutes before slicing. Serves 6 to 8.

Beef Rouladen

Carol Pirozek
Sioux City, IA

*My mother-in-law taught me how to make this recipe. She was
from Germany and they ate this dish often with family &
friends. Now it's a favorite in my family too!*

3 to 4-lb. beef sirloin tip roast
1 lb. bacon, cut in half
2 c. all-purpose flour
8-oz. pkg. sliced mushrooms
1/4 c. oil, divided
3 T. beef soup base

1 c. cornstarch
salt and pepper to taste
mashed potatoes or buttered
   noodles
Garnish: 5 green onion tops,
   chopped

Slice roast into thin strips from the long side, or ask the butcher to
slice. Top each beef slice with a half slice of bacon. Roll up jelly-roll
style; secure with a wooden toothpick. Add flour to a large plastic
zipping bag; place beef rolls inside, a few at a time, and shake to
coat. In a skillet over medium-high heat, sauté mushrooms in
one tablespoon oil; remove and refrigerate. In the same skillet, brown
beef rolls in remaining oil. Arrange beef rolls in a large slow cooker;
add water just to the tops of rolls. Cover and cook on low setting for
6 hours, or until rolls are fork-tender. Remove rolls from slow cooker;
set aside. Pour cooking liquid from the slow cooker into a Dutch oven
over medium heat; stir in beef base. In a bowl, mix cornstarch with
enough hot water to make a thick paste; slowly stir into hot liquid until
mixture thickens. Add beef rolls, salt, pepper and mushrooms to Dutch
oven; heat through. Serve over mashed potatoes or buttered noodles;
garnish with onions. Serves 8 to 10.

For a simple and natural
Christmas decoration, tie
together several twigs with
twine to form primitive stars.

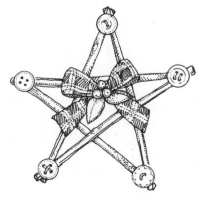

Classic Christmas
❧ Dinner ❧

Easy Slow-Cooker Cornbread Dressing

Angela Montgomery
Jonesboro, AR

This is the dressing we have at all of our family reunions and Thanksgiving dinners. When we walk into the house, we hear tons of laughter and smell the dressing cooking. That's when we know we're home!

8-inch pan cornbread, crumbled
8 slices day-old bread, cubed
1 onion, chopped
1/2 c. celery, chopped
1-1/2 T. dried sage
1 t. salt
1/2 t. pepper
2 10-3/4 oz. cans cream of
   chicken soup
2 14-1/2 oz. cans chicken broth
1 T. margarine, sliced

In a large bowl, combine all ingredients except margarine. Transfer mixture to a greased slow cooker; dot with margarine. Cover and cook on high setting for 2 hours, or on low setting for 3 to 4 hours. Makes 10 servings.

Perhaps this year, one of Santa's elves will make an appearance in your home! Set out a stuffed elf or figurine the day after Thanksgiving to "monitor" good behavior. At night, the elf reports back to the North Pole, and the next morning can usually be found sitting in a different spot.

Best-Ever Stuffing Balls

Barb Rudyk
Alberta, Canada

I always have these savory treats on hand in the freezer...they're quick to reheat for unexpected company!

10 c. dry bread crumbs or
   1 loaf day-old bread, cubed
1/2 c. butter
1 c. celery, finely diced
1 onion, finely diced
10-3/4 oz. can cream of
   mushroom soup

1 t. dried sage
1 t. dried thyme
1 t. salt
1/2 c. fresh parsley, chopped,
   or 1/4 c. dried parsley

Place bread crumbs or cubes in a large bowl. In a skillet over medium heat, melt butter. Sauté celery and onion until tender; add celery mixture to bowl. Add soup and seasonings; mix well. Form mixture into 12 to 14 balls. Place in a greased 13"x9" baking pan; cover with aluminum foil. Bake, covered, at 350 degrees for 25 minutes. Serves 6.

A beautiful, edible garnish for your holiday turkey or ham...crystal cranberries! Just mix 3 cups fresh cranberries with 2 cups sugar and bake, covered, at 300 degrees for one hour, or until berries can be pierced with a fork.

Classic Christmas
❧ Dinner ☙

Ultimate Mashed Potatoes

Judi Towner
Clarks Summit, PA

This is the ultimate recipe for mashed potatoes! Handed down from family to family, it's a dish loved by adults and children alike, asked for at church suppers and insisted upon for holiday dinners.

5 lbs. potatoes, peeled and
    quartered
2 to 3 t. garlic, minced
1 t. salt, or to taste
1/4 c. butter, softened
1 c. sour cream

1/2 c. cream cheese, softened
1 T. Italian salad dressing mix
1/4 t. onion salt
1/4 t. pepper
1/4 c. milk

In a large stockpot, cover potatoes and garlic with water; add salt. Cook over medium-high heat until potatoes are tender, about 20 minutes. Drain; mash potatoes and garlic. Add remaining ingredients; beat with an electric mixer on medium speed until well mixed. Serve immediately. Serves 10.

When the five of us kids were very small, our Grandma Cleo would come over on Christmas Eve to spend the evening with us. One Christmas Eve, unbeknownst to us kids, Dad had slipped outside. Grandma was telling us a story about her Christmas memories, and all of a sudden we heard bells and noises on the roof! Mom told us we needed to get to our beds because Santa was checking to see if it was clear for him to pay his visit. We moved so fast, we just left Grandma sitting there all alone! I'm now 61 years old and I still listen on Christmas Eve to hear the bells.

–Pam Moody, Ashville, OH

Green Bean & Wild Mushroom Casserole

Sharon Demers
Dolores, CO

*This different take on green bean casserole has become
a family tradition at our home.*

3 c. milk
1 bay leaf
1/2 c. butter, divided
1/4 c. all-purpose flour
1/4 t. Dijon mustard
nutmeg to taste
salt and pepper to taste
1 c. shredded white Cheddar
   cheese

1-1/2 c. fresh green beans, cut
   into 2-inch pieces, blanched
   or steamed
3 c. mushrooms such as
   portabella, cremini or
   shiitake, sliced
1/2 c. soft bread crumbs
1/2 c. shredded Parmesan
   cheese

In a saucepan over medium-high heat, bring milk and bay leaf nearly
to a boil. Meanwhile, in another saucepan over medium heat, melt
1/4 cup butter. Add flour to butter and cook, whisking constantly, for
2 minutes. Remove bay leaf from milk; slowly add milk to butter
mixture, whisking constantly. Stir in mustard, nutmeg, salt and
pepper. Cook, stirring occasionally, until thickened, about 5 minutes.
Remove from heat; add Cheddar cheese and stir until cheese is melted.
Fold in green beans and mushrooms; transfer to a buttered 2-quart
casserole dish. Melt remaining butter; toss with bread crumbs. Sprinkle
Parmesan cheese and bread crumbs over casserole. Bake, uncovered,
at 350 degrees for 50 minutes, or until bubbly and golden. Serves 8.

It's fun to mix & match...set a
festive table with items you already
have! Green transferware serving
bowls and jadite cake stands,
sparkling white porcelain dinner
plates and ruby-red stemmed
glasses combine beautifully
with Christmas dinnerware.

Classic Christmas
❦ Dinner ❧

Best Broccoli Casserole

Nancy Kaiser
York, SC

We have this casserole at every holiday meal. It's amazing!

1 to 2 lbs. broccoli, chopped	2 c. milk
6 T. butter, divided	8-oz. pkg. cream cheese, cubed
1/4 c. all-purpose flour	1 c. shredded Cheddar cheese
1/4 t. salt	2 c. soft bread crumbs

In a large saucepan over medium heat, cook broccoli in water until tender; drain and transfer to an ungreased 13"x9" baking pan. In the same saucepan, melt 4 tablespoons butter. Add flour and salt; mix well. Add milk, stirring constantly, until mixture is thick and bubbly. Reduce heat; add cream cheese and stir until smooth. Pour butter mixture over broccoli; mix lightly. Top with Cheddar cheese. Melt remaining butter and toss with bread crumbs; sprinkle over top. Bake, uncovered, at 350 degrees for 40 to 50 minutes, until heated through. Serves 6 to 8.

Baked Spinach Supreme

Kathie Moss
Saint Louis, MO

Delicious...even spinach haters like it!

10-oz. pkg. frozen chopped spinach, thawed and drained	1 c. shredded Cheddar cheese
1 T. onion, minced	1 c. sour cream
1/2 c. tomato sauce	4-oz. can mushroom stems and pieces, drained

Combine all ingredients; transfer to a greased 2-quart casserole dish. Bake, uncovered, at 350 degrees for 30 to 40 minutes, until hot and bubbly. Serves 4 to 6.

For a quick and yummy cheese sauce for veggies, combine one cup evaporated milk and 1/2 cup shredded cheese. Stir over low heat until smooth.

Creamy Mac & Cheese

Gabrielle Wanless
Blanchester, OH

This is my favorite homemade mac & cheese recipe. Unlike most mac & cheese dishes, it gets better as it cools! This would be great made a day before and warmed up later.

2 c. elbow macaroni, uncooked
1/2 c. butter
1/4 c. all-purpose flour
1-1/2 c. milk
8-oz. container sour cream
8-oz. pkg. American cheese
   slices, chopped

1/2 c. grated Parmesan cheese,
   divided
1/2 t. salt
1/2 t. dry mustard
2 c. shredded Cheddar cheese

Cook macaroni according to package instructions; drain and place in a greased 2-quart casserole dish. Meanwhile, in a saucepan over medium heat, melt butter; add flour and milk, stirring until mixture thickens. Reduce heat; add sour cream, American cheese, 1/4 cup Parmesan cheese, salt and mustard. Simmer, stirring constantly, until cheese is melted. Add Cheddar cheese to macaroni; toss. Pour butter mixture over macaroni; mix well. Sprinkle with remaining Parmesan cheese. Bake, uncovered, at 350 degrees for 30 to 40 minutes, until bubbly and golden. Serves 8.

Welcome guests with a line of Mason jar luminarias along your front walk. Simply fill jars half full with rock salt and nestle tea lights in the salt. The flames will make the salt sparkle like ice crystals.

Classic Christmas
❧ Dinner ☙

Cauliflower Gratin

Denise Webb
Galveston, IN

A dear friend of mine brought this dish to our holiday dinner and it was so good it almost outshone the turkey! I had to have seconds and still wanted more. It is an elegant addition to any holiday table.

1 head cauliflower, chopped
6 T. butter
1/4 lb. prosciutto or smoked
    ham, chopped
2 T. all-purpose flour
1-1/2 c. whipping cream

1/8 t. cayenne pepper
2 c. shredded Swiss, Fontina,
    Havarti or Gruyère cheese
2 T. fresh parsley, chopped
1/2 c. round buttery crackers,
    crushed

Fill a large saucepan halfway with water. Bring to a boil; add cauliflower. Return to a boil; cook for 15 minutes, or until cauliflower is tender. Drain; transfer to a greased 2-quart casserole dish. In a large skillet over medium heat, melt butter. Sauté prosciutto or ham in butter for 2 minutes. Stir in flour; add cream and cayenne pepper and bring to a boil. Pour over cauliflower; stir. Sprinkle with cheese; top with parsley and cracker crumbs. Bake, uncovered, at 350 degrees for 30 minutes, or until bubbly and golden. Serves 6 to 8.

Placecards and guest favors all in one! Tape a placecard to the wire loop at the top of a tree ornament, and then lay one at each place setting. Guests can take the ornament home as a reminder of all the fun they had.

Nancy's Green Bean Casserole
Nancy Heesch
Sioux Falls, SD

*This is our family's most-requested dish come holiday time.
I created this recipe when I was bored with the familiar
green bean casserole recipe.*

15-1/2 oz. can French-style
  green beans, drained
3-1/2 oz. can French fried
  onions
10-3/4 oz. can cream of chicken
  soup

1/2 c. milk
1/2 t. dried basil
1/2 c. shredded sharp Cheddar
  cheese
3 slices bacon, partially cooked
  and cut into thirds

Spread half the green beans in an ungreased 2-quart casserole dish;
top with half the onions. Repeat layers. In a bowl, mix soup, milk and
basil; pour over onions. Top with cheese and bacon pieces. Bake,
uncovered, at 375 degrees for 35 to 40 minutes, until hot and bubbly.
Serves 4 to 6.

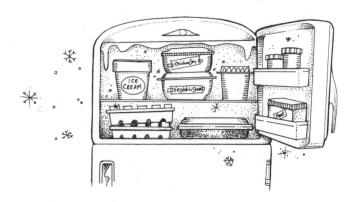

When cooking for Christmas, make use of your freezer. You can
prepare soups weeks in advance and freeze them until you are
ready to serve them, garnished with a dollop of cream. They're an
elegant yet simple appetizer for your holiday meal.

Classic Christmas
🍃 Dinner 🍃

Sausage & Squash Casserole
Ann Smith
Columbus, OH

I've served this recipe to family & friends at many potlucks and it's always enjoyed. I started making it as a means to use up the many butternut squash from my garden.

1 butternut squash, peeled and
  cubed
1/2 c. brown sugar, packed
1 lb. ground pork sausage

1 onion, diced
2 stalks celery, diced
3/4 c. water
3 c. stuffing mix

Place squash in a microwave-safe bowl; cover with plastic wrap. Microwave on high setting for 20 minutes, or until squash is tender. Stir brown sugar into squash. In a skillet over medium heat, brown sausage with onion and celery; drain. Add water and dry stuffing mix to skillet; mix well. Combine all ingredients in a microwave-safe 2-quart casserole dish. Microwave on high setting for 15 minutes, or until heated through. Serves 6 to 8.

Cinnamon Apples
Kimberly Marlatt
Yuma, AZ

My one goal for Christmas Day was not to spend the whole day in the kitchen. You can make these delicious apples a couple of days in advance and just reheat them in the microwave!

2 T. butter
4 apples, peeled, cored and
  sliced

1/3 c. brown sugar, packed
2 T. lemon juice
3/4 t. cinnamon

In a saucepan over medium heat, melt butter. Add remaining ingredients; cook and stir until apples are golden and soft. Serve immediately, or cover and refrigerate until ready to serve. Serves 4 to 6.

To create a special touch for overnight guests, stack red, white or green bath towels in the guest bath and tie them with wide ribbon.

Red-Top Salad

Penny Rehder
North Richland Hills, TX

Whenever I make this wonderful salad, I always think of my grandmother preparing it. It's so delicious that it could be a dessert. I guarantee that Red-Top Salad will be a big hit with everyone, so you may want to double or even triple the recipe!

20-oz. can crushed pineapple, drained and juice reserved
3-oz. pkg. lemon gelatin mix
1 c. whipping cream
1/2 c. cream cheese, softened
1/2 c. celery, chopped
1/2 c. chopped walnuts or pecans
6-oz. pkg. strawberry gelatin mix

Combine reserved pineapple juice with enough water to make one cup. In a saucepan over medium heat, bring juice mixture to a boil. Add lemon gelatin mix; stir until dissolved. Refrigerate. Meanwhile, in a chilled bowl with an electric mixer on medium speed, whip cream until soft peaks form. Beat in cream cheese, blending well. Fold in celery, nuts and pineapple. When lemon gelatin begins to set, fold it into cream mixture, blending well. Transfer cream mixture to a 13"x9" baking pan; refrigerate until firm. Meanwhile, prepare strawberry gelatin mix according to package directions. Refrigerate gelatin just until it begins to set; pour over chilled cream mixture. Cover; refrigerate until firm. Keep chilled. Serves 6 to 8.

Festive Holiday Fare

Bread-Bowl Crab Dip

Stefanie St. Pierre
South Dennis, MA

A delicious dip that always gets rave reviews! Baked and served in a bread bowl, this recipe is quick & easy to make.

2 6-oz. cans crabmeat, drained
  and flaked
8-oz. container whipped cream
  cheese
1 T. prepared horseradish

1 to 2 green onions, finely
  chopped
Worcestershire sauce to taste
salt and pepper to taste
1 round bread loaf

In a bowl, combine all ingredients except bread; blend well. Cut a hole in the top of the bread loaf; carefully remove the insides. Cut removed bread into cubes; set aside. Spoon crabmeat mixture into bread loaf and place in an ungreased baking pan. Bake at 375 degrees for 20 to 30 minutes, until dip is bubbly and golden on top. Serve with cubed bread for dipping. Serves 4 to 6.

This veggie-packed topiary will certainly "spruce" up your buffet table! Cover a 12-inch styrofoam cone with aluminum foil. Attach broccoli flowerets and cherry tomatoes by sticking one end of a toothpick into the veggie and the other end into the cone. Garnish with cheese "ornaments" cut out with mini cookie cutters...clever!

Festive Holiday Fare

Spectacular Bruschetta

Nancy Girard
Chesapeake, VA

This is the best bruschetta I have ever had. I make it for parties or special occasions. If you have any leftover tomato mixture, try serving it on top of fettuccine Alfredo!

6 roma tomatoes, chopped
1/2 c. sun-dried tomatoes,
   packed in oil
3 cloves garlic, minced
1/4 c. olive oil
2 T. balsamic vinegar
1/4 c. fresh basil, chopped

1/4 t. salt
1/4 t. pepper
1 French baguette, sliced
   3/4-inch thick
2 c. shredded mozzarella cheese
Optional: grated Parmesan
   cheese

In a large bowl, combine tomatoes, garlic, olive oil, vinegar, basil, salt and pepper. Allow mixture to stand for 10 minutes, or make ahead and refrigerate until serving time. On a baking sheet, arrange bread slices in a single layer. Broil for one to 2 minutes, until lightly golden and toasted. Divide tomato mixture evenly over bread slices. Top with mozzarella cheese. Sprinkle with Parmesan cheese, if desired. Broil for 5 minutes longer, or until cheese melts. Serve immediately. Serves 12.

For twinkling lights with added country charm, tie fabric strips or ribbons onto a strand of Christmas lights.

Figgy Tapenade

JoAnn

Because who makes figgy pudding anymore? This is an easy and impressive appetizer. Serve with slices of French bread or crackers.

1 c. dried figs, chopped
1/2 c. water
1 T. olive oil
2 T. balsamic vinegar
1 t. dried rosemary
1 t. dried thyme

1/4 t. cayenne pepper
2/3 c. Kalamata olives, chopped
2 cloves garlic, minced
salt and pepper to taste
8-oz. pkg. cream cheese
1/3 c. toasted walnuts, chopped

Combine figs and water in a saucepan over medium heat. Bring to a boil; cook until figs are tender and liquid has cooked down. Remove from heat; stir in olive oil, vinegar, herbs and cayenne pepper. Add olives and garlic; mix well. Season with salt and pepper. Cover; refrigerate for 4 hours to overnight. To serve, unwrap cream cheese; place on a serving plate. Spoon tapenade over top; sprinkle with walnuts. Serves 6.

Nothing says Christmas like fresh touches of greenery sprinkled throughout your home! When buying a fresh tree, be sure to take home any boughs cut from the base of the tree. You can also ask permission to collect any greens from the ground.

Festive Holiday ❧ **Fare** ❧

Pine Cone Cheese Ball

Frances Mertz
Wilmington, OH

Easy to assemble and looks so pretty for the holidays. A favorite of my family for many years at our annual holiday open house!

2 8-oz. pkgs. cream cheese,
   softened
2 c. shredded sharp Cheddar
   cheese
1 T. chopped pimentos
1 T onion, chopped

1 T. green pepper, chopped
2 t. Worcestershire sauce
1 t. lemon juice
16-oz. pkg. sliced almonds
assorted crackers

In a bowl, combine cheeses; mix well. Add remaining ingredients except almonds and crackers; mix well. Divide cheese mixture into 2 portions. Wrap each tightly in plastic wrap; chill until firm. Form into 2 egg-like shapes; cover each with almonds, pressing in to resemble pine cones. If you wish, decorate with a sprig of artificial greenery. Serve with crackers. Serves 10 to 12.

Every year when my children were growing up, they looked forward to December. We used their Christmas stockings to count down the days till Santa came. I took 24 ribbons of varying lengths and attached a piece of candy or a small treat to the end of each ribbon. Hiding that end of the ribbon in the stocking, I attached numbers 1 through 24 to the other end. Every day each child would pull out a ribbon. They were always so excited to find the treat at the other end. They also loved watching the ribbons disappear because they knew when number 24 was pulled, Santa would come that night! It was such a fun tradition.

–Virginia Craven, Denton, TX

Festive Fireside Meatballs

Janis Parr
Ontario, Canada

This recipe was shared with me many years ago at a potluck with the girls from work. I've tasted lots of meatballs over the years, but these top them all!

2 lbs. lean ground beef
1-oz. pkg. onion soup mix
1 egg, beaten
1/4 c. dry bread crumbs
2 c. brown sugar, packed
10-oz. bottle chili sauce
1-1/4 c. regular or non-alcoholic
   beer

salt and pepper to taste
1/2 t. garlic powder
2 t. Worcestershire sauce
3-1/2 T. cornstarch
1/4 c. cold water

In a large bowl, combine beef, soup mix, egg and bread crumbs; mix well. Roll into walnut-sized balls. In a skillet over medium heat, brown meatballs on all sides. Drain on paper towels. In a large saucepan over medium heat, combine remaining ingredients except cornstarch and water. Bring to a boil. Stir cornstarch into cold water; gradually add to mixture in saucepan and cook until thickened. Place meatballs in saucepan; stir to coat. Simmer over low heat for about one hour, or until glazed. Serves 8 to 10.

Create a showcase for your favorite
Christmas ornaments by perching
them atop assorted candlesticks.
Keep fragile ornaments stable
by using a dab of museum
wax to anchor them
to the candlesticks.

Festive Holiday Fare

Snow-Covered Cranberries

Robin Thompson
Wylie, TX

This is a really simple and remarkably delicious treat.
Serve in a pretty bowl and enjoy!

12-oz. pkg. fresh cranberries   2 c. powdered sugar

Sort cranberries and rinse well. While cranberries are still moist, roll them in powdered sugar until well coated. Serves 10 to 15.

Giant peppermint stick decorations...over-the-top outdoor decorations the kids will love! Go to your carpet store and ask for the cardboard tubes that carpet comes on...they usually get tossed out. Paint them with white spray paint or wrap them in white paper or plastic and twist with red ribbon.

Turtle Cheese Ball

Kim McCallie
Guyton, GA

What is better than the flavors in a candy turtle?
Chocolate, pecans and caramel...yummy!

8-oz. pkg. cream cheese,
  softened
1/4 c. butter, softened
1/3 c. powdered sugar
1/2 c. brown sugar, packed
1 t. vanilla extract

1 c. toffee baking bits
1 c. mini semi-sweet chocolate
  chips
Optional: 1 c. chopped pecans
graham crackers, apple slices

In a bowl, beat cream cheese and butter until smooth. Add powdered sugar, brown sugar and vanilla; blend until smooth. Stir in toffee bits and chocolate chips. Refrigerate mixture for about 30 minutes, or until it starts to firm up. Remove from bowl; spoon mixture onto a sheet of plastic wrap and form into a ball. Wrap tightly; refrigerate overnight. Before serving, unwrap ball and press pecans into the ball, if using. Serve with graham crackers or apple slices. Serves 10 to 12.

For an arrangement that's sure to please, place a Turtle Cheese Ball in the center of a snowy-white plate and surround it with rings of red and green apple slices. Be sure to dip the apple wedges in lemon juice first to keep them from turning brown.

Festive Holiday Fare

Cannoli Dip

Lauren Schoener-Gaynor
Cherry Hill, NJ

This recipe was shared with me by one of my husband's cousins. As proud Italians, this dip is a family staple. Although it doesn't include ricotta cheese like traditional cannolis, it definitely gives you your cannoli fix if you can't get to your favorite Italian bakery.

8-oz. pkg. cream cheese,
  softened
1/2 c. butter, softened
3/4 c. powdered sugar
1 t. vanilla extract

3/4 c. mini semi-sweet chocolate
  chips
Optional: 3/4 c. chopped pecans
broken cannoli shells or
  cinnamon-sugar pita chips

In a bowl, beat cream cheese and butter until fluffy. Add sugar, vanilla and chocolate chips, mixing well after each addition. Shape mixture into a ball; wrap tightly in plastic wrap. Refrigerate for at least 2 hours before serving. Before serving, unwrap ball and roll in pecans before serving. Serve with broken cannoli shells or cinnamon-sugar pita chips. Serves 8 to 10.

If a recipe calls for softened butter, grate chilled sticks with a cheese grater. The butter will soften in just minutes.

Peppery Olive Focaccia

Eleanor Dionne
Beverly, MA

My daughter loves making this and everyone loves eating it. Yummy!

2 1-lb. loaves frozen bread
   dough, thawed
2 T. olive oil
2 cloves garlic, minced
1/3 c. black or green olives,
   chopped

1/8 to 1/4 t. red pepper flakes
1 t. fresh rosemary, minced, or
   1/2 t. dried rosemary
1/2 c. shredded Parmesan
   cheese

Lightly grease a 15"x10" jelly-roll pan. Pat and stretch dough to fit into pan. Drizzle with olive oil. Sprinkle with remaining ingredients. Allow to rise at room temperature for one hour. Bake at 375 degrees for 12 to 14 minutes, until golden. Cut into squares. Serves 8 to 12.

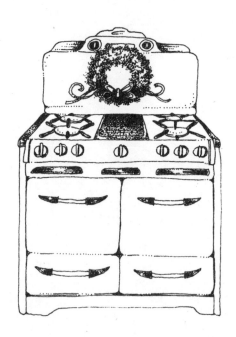

A 250-degree oven keeps hot appetizers toasty
until you're ready to serve them.

Festive Holiday Fare

Blue Cheese & Buffalo Chicken Dip

Lori Haines
Johnson City, TN

My son can eat a whole batch of this dip at once, so if his father or I want any, I have to double the recipe! It's yummy with celery sticks.

8-oz. pkg. cream cheese, softened
1/2 c. blue cheese salad dressing
1/2 c. favorite-flavor mild or hot pepper sauce
1/2 c. blue cheese crumbles
2 12-1/2 oz. cans chicken breast, drained
1 c. shredded Mexican-blend cheese
crackers, tortilla scoops or sliced veggies

In a bowl, combine cream cheese, salad dressing and hot sauce. Fold in blue cheese and chicken. Spread in an ungreased 8"x8" baking pan; sprinkle with shredded cheese. Bake, uncovered, at 350 degrees for about 20 minutes, or until bubbly. Serve warm with crackers, tortilla scoops or veggies. Serves 8 to 12.

A simple accent for a dining table, a fireplace mantel or a long console table...take any assortment of glass bottles and spray-paint them holiday colors. Fill with candles, flowers or twigs for a festive touch.

New Year's Wings

Valerie Hendrickson
Cedar Springs, MI

*A long-standing holiday tradition! The recipe came to us
from good family friends. It wouldn't be Christmas or
New Year's without these wings. Delicious!*

4-oz. bottle low-sodium soy
    sauce
8-oz. bottle zesty Italian salad
    dressing

12-oz. bottle pure maple syrup
4 to 5 lbs. chicken wings,
    thawed if frozen

In a bowl, combine soy sauce, salad dressing and syrup. Divide wings
between 2 large plastic zipping bags; add half of soy sauce mixture to
each bag, turning to coat wings. Refrigerate for 2 to 24 hours. Transfer
wings with marinade into 2 ungreased 13"x9" baking pans. Bake,
uncovered, at 325 degrees for 2 hours. Increase oven to 375 degrees;
bake for 30 minutes longer, turning and coating wings every
10 minutes. Serves 6 to 8.

Mini potted evergreen trees are a fun alternative to
poinsettias or houseplants...plus, you can decorate
them with your tiniest ornaments.

Festive Holiday Fare

Sauerkraut Balls

Lisa Burns
Findlay, OH

*My parents always made these golden & savory
treats for the holidays.*

1 lb. ground pork sausage
1/2 c. onion, minced
26-oz. can sauerkraut, drained
  and chopped
3/4 c. dry bread crumbs, divided
8-oz. pkg. cream cheese,
  softened

1/4 c. fresh parsley, minced
2 t. mustard
2 T. garlic salt
3 eggs, beaten
1/2 c. milk
1/2 c. all-purpose flour
shortening for deep frying

In a skillet over medium heat, brown sausage and onion; drain. In a
large bowl, combine sausage mixture, sauerkraut and 1/4 cup bread
crumbs; mix well. In a separate bowl, combine cream cheese, parsley,
mustard and garlic salt; stir into sausage mixture. Shape into
3/4-inch balls. In a shallow bowl, combine eggs and milk; place flour
in a separate bowl. Coat balls in flour; dip into egg mixture. Roll in
remaining bread crumbs. Let balls stand until they reach room
temperature. In a deep fryer or extra-deep skillet, melt enough
shortening to create a one-inch depth. Heat to 375 degrees. Fry balls
in small batches for 10 to 12 minutes, turning to cook on all sides,
until golden and cooked through. Drain on paper towels. Serves 12.

I wish we could put up some of the Christmas spirit
in jars and open a jar of it every month.

–Harlan Miller

Spinach Dip Provencal

Ursula Juarez-Wall
Dumfries, VA

I never bring home any leftovers whenever I bring this hearty appetizer to potlucks! A wonderfully rustic dip that can also be served with sourdough bread.

1/2 c. pine nuts
2 T. olive oil
1 red onion, finely chopped
1-1/2 T. fresh thyme, chopped
11-oz. pkg. goat cheese, room
   temperature
1-1/2 c. milk

10-oz. pkg frozen spinach,
   thawed, drained and finely
   chopped
10 Kalamata olives, chopped
2 cloves garlic, minced
1/2 t. lemon juice
salt and pepper to taste

Spread pine nuts on an ungreased baking sheet; bake at 400 degrees for about 4 minutes, until golden. Set aside. Meanwhile, in a large skillet, warm olive oil over medium-high heat. Add onion and thyme; reduce heat to low. Cook, stirring occasionally, until onion is tender and golden, about 10 minutes. Set aside. In a bowl, mash goat cheese with a fork until creamy. Gradually blend in milk. Fold in spinach, olives, garlic, onion mixture and pine nuts. Add lemon juice; season with salt and pepper. Serve with Savory Toasts. Serves 8 to 12.

Savory Toasts:

1 loaf French bread, sliced
   1/4-inch thick
2 T. olive oil

1 t. dried Greek oregano or
   herbs de Provence

Lightly brush one side of each bread slice with olive oil. Arrange slices, oiled-side up, on a baking sheet. Bake until golden, about 5 minutes. Sprinkle with herbs.

Festive Holiday Fare

Mushroom Poppers

Julianne Saifullah
Lexington, KY

It's the best of both worlds...a stuffed mushroom and jalapeño popper in one tasty bite!

16 mushrooms
2 cloves garlic, minced
2 jalapeño peppers, finely chopped, ribs and seeds removed
1 T. olive oil
2 3-oz. pkgs. cream cheese, softened

1/4 c. plus 2 T. shredded Cheddar cheese
4 slices bacon, crisply cooked and crumbled
salt and pepper to taste

Separate mushroom stems from caps; set caps aside. Finely chop stems. In a skillet over medium heat, cook chopped stems, garlic and peppers in oil; cook and stir until mushrooms are tender, about 10 minutes. Transfer mushroom mixture to a bowl; stir in cheeses and bacon. Season with salt and pepper. Spoon mushroom mixture generously into reserved mushroom caps; arrange caps in a lightly greased 13"x9" baking pan. Bake, uncovered, at 350 degrees for 15 to 20 minutes, until golden on top. Serves 8.

Upgrade your glass of bubbly! To one flute of champagne or sparkling white grape juice, add your choice of one tablespoon pomegranate juice, one scoop mango sorbet, one tablespoon grapefruit juice or one teaspoon amaretto liqueur.

Sausage Stars

Tina Butler
Royse City, TX

Everyone has looked forward to these yummy little appetizers at our all our family gatherings for a long time. This is the first treat we all grab from the table.

1 lb. ground pork sausage
1-oz. pkg. ranch salad dressing
  mix
8-oz. pkg. shredded Mexican-
  blend cheese

Optional: 1/2 c. green or red
  pepper, chopped
12-oz. pkg. wonton wrappers or
  egg roll wrappers

Brown sausage in a skillet over medium-high heat; drain and set aside. Prepare salad dressing mix according to package directions. Combine cooled sausage, dressing, cheese and pepper, if using; chill for 30 minutes. Place one wonton wrapper into each cup of a lightly greased muffin tin. Push down gently to form a little shell-like cup. Bake 5 to 7 minutes, just until lightly golden. Watch carefully; do not allow cups to turn brown. Remove from oven; let cool. Fill each cup with about 2 tablespoons of sausage mixture. Bake 5 to 7 minutes longer, until cheese melts. Cool before serving. Makes about 4 dozen.

Turn your holiday cards into a Christmas garland...a great party decoration! Use mini clothespins to clip cards to a length of ribbon or twine. Add some favorite holiday photos and handmade gift tags to create a heartfelt display that family & friends are sure to enjoy.

Festive Holiday ❧ **Fare** ❧

Holiday Shrimp Butter

Karen Crooks
West Des Moines, IA

A good friend gave me this recipe 30 years ago. It is now a yearly holiday tradition, and my daughter expects it every Christmas Eve! It can be prepared ahead and kept in the freezer for several weeks...a wonderful time-saver for holiday entertaining.

2 5-oz. cans small shrimp, drained and rinsed
1/4 c. mayonnaise-type salad dressing or mayonnaise
1 T. onion, minced
3/4 c. butter, softened

8-oz. pkg. cream cheese, softened
1 T. lemon juice
round buttery crackers or toasted baguette slices

Combine all ingredients except crackers or baguette slices in a bowl; beat with an electric mixer on low speed until fluffy. Serve with crackers or baguette slices. Serves 8.

Beer Cheese Spread

Nancy Gasko
South Bend, IN

Serve this spicy spread with pretzels for a tasty game-time snack. If there are any leftovers, spread on buttered bread and grill for a delicious twist on the traditional grilled cheese sandwich.

2 8-oz. pkgs. cream cheese, softened
1-oz. pkg. ranch salad dressing mix

2 c. finely shredded Cheddar cheese
1/3 c. regular or non-alcoholic beer

Beat cream cheese and salad dressing mix in a bowl with an electric mixer on low speed. Add cheese and beer; mix well. Chill for 3 hours to overnight. Makes about 4 cups.

Spoon dips and spreads into pretty crocks or vintage blue canning jars...they're ideal as hostess gifts. Don't forget to tie on a spreader too!

BBQ Wontons

Haley Carroll
Billings, MT

These adorable wontons are absolutely delicious and savory. If you make these for a party, double the recipe...they will go fast!

1/2 lb. ground beef or pork
1/4 c. green onions, chopped
1 t. dried, minced onion
2 cloves garlic, minced
2 T. plus 1/4 c. favorite-flavor
    barbecue sauce, divided
1 t. Dijon mustard
1/4 t. paprika

1/4 t. sugar
salt and pepper to taste
Worcestershire sauce and hot
    pepper sauce to taste
25 to 30 wonton wrappers
canola oil for frying
2/3 c. chicken broth, divided

In a bowl, combine meat, onions, garlic, 2 tablespoons barbecue sauce, mustard, seasonings and sauces; blend well. Lay wonton wrappers out, 6 at a time. Dip a finger into a bowl of warm water and outline outer edges of wrapper with water. Place one rounded teaspoon of meat mixture in the center of each wrapper; top with a dash of remaining barbecue sauce. Pinch together opposite corners of each wrapper. Bring remaining sides of wrapper to center; pinch and twist top to finish. Once wontons are assembled, add oil to just cover the bottom of a skillet. Heat oil over medium heat. Add half of wontons. Cook, uncovered, bottoms only, for 2 minutes. Carefully add 1/3 cup chicken broth. Cover and steam for 3 minutes. Remove wontons from pan. Empty skillet; repeat steps for remaining wontons. Serve with remaining barbecue sauce for dipping. Makes 2 to 2-1/2 dozen.

Chalkboard gift pots...clever holders for gifts of herb plants or serving bread sticks on the dinner table. Paint terra-cotta flowerpots with green or black chalkboard paint, then write a holiday greeting on them.

Festive Holiday **Fare**

Japanese-Style Chicken Wings
Goreta Brown
Alberta, Canada

These wings have crispy exteriors and lots of flavor!

30 chicken wings
1 c. all-purpose flour
salt and pepper to taste
1 egg, beaten
1/2 c. butter
1/2 c. oil

3 T. soy sauce
3 T. water
1 c. sugar
1/2 c. vinegar
1/2 t. salt
1 T. red pepper flakes

Pat wings dry with a paper towel. In a shallow bowl, combine flour with salt and pepper; place egg in a separate bowl. Dip wings in egg, then in flour mixture. In a skillet over medium-high heat, melt butter and add oil; fry wings in butter mixture, turning often, until crisp. Drain and pat off excess oil. Transfer wings to an ungreased 13"x9" baking pan. In a bowl, combine remaining ingredients. Drizzle mixture over wings. Bake, uncovered, at 350 degrees for about 45 minutes, tossing wings several times, until liquid evaporates and wings are crisp and cooked through. Serve hot. Serves 6 to 8.

My grown kids live on opposite sides of the country, Pennsylvania and Washington state, so they don't get to see one another often. And because of their schedules, we don't always get to celebrate Christmas on the actual day. As my mother used to say, "Christmas is when we're all together." So, sometimes Christmas is in October, and sometimes it's in January. But when we're all together, I just love to sit back and listen to them...the banter, the joking, the teasing, the laughing...I love it! I take it all in and when I miss seeing them, I bring up these memories.

–Bonnie Scholtes, Orwigsburg, PA

Cheddar Fondue

Kristy Markners
Fort Mill, SC

We love making fondue and serving it with a variety of dippers.
It's a fun appetizer to serve at parties!

2-1/2 c. shredded extra-sharp
   Cheddar cheese
1-1/2 c. shredded Swiss cheese
1 T. all-purpose flour
12-oz. bottle beer or
   1-1/2 c. broth
1/2 t. Worcestershire sauce

1/2 t. dry mustard
hot pepper sauce to taste
variety of dippers, such as
   bread cubes, lightly steamed
   veggies or apple slices

In a bowl, toss cheeses with flour; set aside. In a saucepan over medium heat, bring beer or broth to a slow boil. Reduce heat to a simmer. Slowly stir in cheese mixture, stirring constantly. When cheese is fully melted, stir in Worcestershire sauce, mustard and hot sauce. Transfer to a warmed fondue pot. Serve with dippers. Serves 8.

Put an old-fashioned wooden ladder to use as a display for some of your most treasured Christmas ornaments.

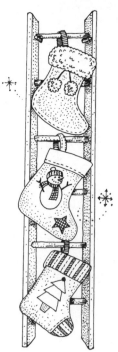

Festive Holiday Fare

Festive Mushroom Puffs

Ramona Storm
Gardner, IL

These tasty morsels always get eaten up very fast! The filling can be made ahead and refrigerated...a real time-saver.

1/2 c. cream cheese, softened
4-oz. can mushroom stems &
  pieces, drained
1 green onion, chopped

1/8 t. hot pepper sauce
8-oz. tube refrigerated crescent
  rolls

In a bowl with an electric mixer on medium speed, beat cream cheese, mushrooms, onion and pepper sauce; blend well. Separate crescent roll dough into 4 rectangles, pressing to seal perforations. Spread cream cheese mixture over rolls. Roll up dough jelly-roll style, starting with the long side. With a serrated knife, cut each roll into 5 slices. Place on an ungreased baking sheet. Bake at 425 degrees for 8 to 10 minutes, until lightly golden. Makes 20.

Hot Cheese Puffs

Susie Clayton
Henderson, NV

I've been serving this easy appetizer since I was a newlywed 30 years ago. Often I double the recipe because they disappear in a jiffy!

4-oz. container spreadable garlic
  & herbs soft cheese
10 slices soft white bread, crusts
  removed

1/2 c. butter, melted
3/4 c. grated Parmesan cheese

Spread cheese over bread slices. Roll up jelly-roll style; cut each into 3 pieces. Dip each piece in butter, then dredge in Parmesan cheese. Place on a greased baking sheet. Bake at 425 degrees for 7 to 8 minutes, until golden. Serve immediately. Makes 2-1/2 dozen.

Spoon creamy ranch dip into short plastic tumblers and add crunchy celery stalks, red pepper strips and carrot sticks. Nestle the cups in a tray of ice. Oh-so easy for guests to pick up and carry around at a party!

Evergreen Cheese Ball

Jill Ross
Gooseberry Patch

*Mix up this cheese ball the day before so the flavors can blend.
Sometimes I shape it into a festive cone-shaped "tree" for Christmas,
but it's definitely a crowd-pleaser all year 'round!*

3 T. pecans, finely chopped
8-oz. pkg. cream cheese,
  softened
1/3 c. green onion, finely
  chopped
1 t. Dijon mustard

1/4 t. hot pepper sauce
1/4 t. garlic, minced
1 c. sharp Cheddar cheese,
  shredded
1/4 c. fresh parsley, minced

In a baking pan, toast pecans at 350 degrees for 8 minutes, tossing once. Meanwhile, in a bowl, combine cream cheese, onion, mustard, pepper sauce and garlic; beat with an electric mixer on medium speed for 3 minutes, or until well blended. Stir in Cheddar cheese. Shape mixture into a ball; wrap tightly in plastic wrap. Chill for 15 minutes. On a sheet of wax paper, toss pecans with parsley. Unwrap cheese ball and carefully roll it in the pecan mixture, coating completely. Rewrap loosely in plastic wrap and refrigerate until serving time. Serves 10 to 12.

If your fireplace isn't used during the holidays, it can still look warm and inviting. Fill an empty grate with cheerful wrapped packages, candles of every shape and size or snowy-white birch logs accented by shiny ornaments.

Festive Holiday
Fare

Raspberry Brie Tarts

Debbie Cutelli
Saint Louis, MO

These tarts look amazing on a holiday platter! I always keep the ingredients on hand to make this appetizer in case friends drop in.

2 2.1-oz. pkgs. frozen mini
   phyllo shells
8-oz. round Brie cheese, cut into
   1/2-inch cubes

3 T. raspberry spreadable fruit

Place phyllo shells on a large ungreased baking sheet. Place 3 cheese cubes into each shell. Bake at 350 degrees for 10 to 12 minutes, until cheese is melted and bubbly. Remove from oven. Spoon 1/4 teaspoon fruit over cheese in each shell. Return to oven; bake an additional 2 to 3 minutes, until heated through. Serve warm. Makes about 30.

Mini Chicken Cups

Teresa Eller
Tonganoxie, KS

You can make these tasty chilled cups ahead. Just pop 'em in the fridge and they'll be ready when your guests arrive.

2.1-oz. pkg. frozen mini phyllo
   shells
2 c. cooked chicken, shredded
1/2 c. celery, chopped
1/2 c. chopped pecans

3/4 c. mayonnaise
15 fresh spinach leaves,
   trimmed
Garnish: paprika or chili powder
   to taste

Bake phyllo shells according to package directions. In a bowl, mix chicken, celery, pecans and mayonnaise. Place one spinach leaf in each cup. Divide chicken mixture evenly among cups; sprinkle with paprika or chili powder. Serve chilled. Makes 15.

For a quick & easy Christmas decoration with a big impact, frame some cheery wrapping paper or favorite holiday fabrics and hang on the wall.

Festive Veggie Flatbreads

Vickie

This veggie-packed appetizer will add lots of color to your buffet table.

1-1/4 c. fresh vegetables,
    such as broccoli, carrots,
    red onion, yellow squash,
    mushrooms and peppers,
    finely chopped
1/4 t. salt
1/8 t. pepper

1/4 c. Kalamata olives, chopped
1/4 to 1/2 t. lemon zest
4-oz. container garlic & herbs
    spreadable soft cheese
5 6-inch flatbreads
1 c. shredded Cheddar cheese
1/4 c. Havarti cheese, shredded

In a bowl, combine vegetables, salt, pepper, olives and zest. Spread soft cheese over each flatbread; top with vegetable mixture, pressing in lightly. Sprinkle with Cheddar and Havarti cheeses. Slice each flatbread into 6 wedges to serve. Makes 15 servings.

Growing up, every Christmas Eve we'd turn on a holiday show on TV and while it was playing in the background, we would be in the kitchen with Dad. He'd mix up some sugar cookie dough, and we kids gathered around to cut fun shapes out of the dough. After they were finished baking, we frosted and decorated them. Then we picked out our favorite cookies and put them on a plate to leave out for Santa with a glass of milk. On Christmas morning we would run to the plate to see if Santa had eaten all the cookies. He sure had! This is a tradition I've started with my own young daughter. Christmas Eve is a busy time, so we don't do sugar cookies. But we make a batch of chocolate chip cookies to leave out for Santa with a glass of milk!

–Mary Hammond, Blackfoot, ID

Festive Holiday Fare

Hankering Green Sauce

Cathy Gearheart
Narrows, VA

*This dip is a must at every family get-together! Have the recipe
handy, as I guarantee you'll be asked for it.*

4 avocados, halved, pitted
   and cubed
3-oz. pkg. cream cheese,
   softened
16-oz. container sour cream
1 t. lemon juice

1 T. garlic powder
2 t. salt
10-oz. can diced tomatoes with
   green chiles
4-oz. can diced green chiles
tortilla chips

In a food processor, combine avocados, cream cheese, sour cream,
lemon juice, garlic powder and salt; process until smooth. Add
tomatoes with juice and chiles; pulse several times to finish. Serve
with chips. Serves 20.

Holly Jolly Kabobs

Jill Ball
Highland, UT

*This tasty appetizer makes a colorful addition to your meal. It's so
easy that the kids can help assemble it!*

15 toothpicks
15 cherry or grape tomatoes
1 to 2 green peppers, cut into
   squares

8-oz. pkg. mozzarella cheese,
   cubed
Garnish: Italian salad dressing
   to taste

On each toothpick, skewer one tomato, one piece green pepper and
one cheese cube. Place on a serving plate; drizzle with salad dressing.
Makes 15.

Put the kids to work rolling up party-
portable flatware in colorful napkins.
Tie bundles with red and white
bakers' twine and stack them
in a flat basket.

Parmesan Toasts

Melinda Nau
Florence, KY

This is an incredibly easy appetizer recipe that I can whip up quickly when unexpected guests surprise us.

1 loaf French bread, thinly sliced   1/2 c. grated Parmesan cheese
1/2 c. mayonnaise

Place bread slices on a baking sheet; bake at 400 degrees until toasted, about 5 minutes. Meanwhile, in a bowl, combine mayonnaise and cheese. Spread some cheese mixture on each toast. Return to baking sheet; broil under low heat until cheese is golden and bubbly. Serve immediately. Serves 12.

Bacon-Wrapped Dates

Marcia Marcoux
Charlton, MA

So simple and delicious.

1 lb. bacon   Optional: 25 to 30 wooden
8 to 12-oz. pkg. pitted whole   toothpicks
   dates

Cut bacon slices into thirds. Wrap a piece of bacon around each date. Secure with a toothpick, if using, or wrap tightly and place seam-side down on an ungreased baking sheet. Bake at 350 degrees for 20 to 25 minutes, until bacon is crisp. Cool 10 to 15 minutes before serving. Makes 2 to 2-1/2 dozen.

Easily remove the melted wax from your favorite holiday candleholders. Just put them in the freezer for a couple of hours, and the wax will pop right out!

Festive Holiday
Fare

Betty's Spiced Pecans

Naomi Townsend
Ozark, MO

When my daughter was in Sunday School, her teacher gave each family a small jar of these pecans for Christmas. I've been making them every year since!

1 egg white
1 t. water
4 c. pecan halves
3/4 c. sugar

1 T. pumpkin pie spice
1 t. salt
1 t. butter

In a bowl with an electric mixer on high speed, beat egg white until stiff peaks form. Stir in water. Add pecans; toss to coat. In a small bowl, combine sugar, spice and salt. Add to pecans; toss until well coated. Line a baking sheet with aluminum foil; coat with butter. Arrange nuts in a single layer on foil. Bake at 300 degrees for 20 to 25 minutes. Cool before breaking apart. Store in an airtight container. Makes 16 to 20 servings.

Cinnamon-Spice Popcorn

Melinda Hochstettler
Cookeville, TN

Sitting around the fireplace and munching on our favorite snack is a holiday tradition! Growing up, there were eight of us kids. We lived without electricity and Mom cooked on a great big wood stove. She still does today whenever we get together at the homeplace.

3 T. butter
1/2 t. cinnamon
1/4 t. nutmeg

2 T. sugar
8 c. popcorn, popped

In a saucepan over medium heat, melt butter slowly; gently mix in spices and sugar. Stir until sugar is dissolved and mixture is smooth. Place popcorn in a large heatproof bowl. Pour butter mixture over popcorn; toss and stir until all pieces are coated. Makes about 8 cups.

Brandy Slush

Sue Klapper
Muskego, WI

I first had this frosty drink more than 40 years ago. My aunt's elderly tenant came to a party carrying a large ice cream pail. I never suspected its contents: Brandy Slush! I've since made it for countless gatherings.

9 c. water, divided
2 c. sugar
4 teabags
12-oz. can frozen orange juice
    concentrate

12-oz. frozen lemonade
    concentrate
2 c. brandy
1-ltr. bottle lemon-lime soda,
    chilled

In a large saucepan over high heat, bring 7 cups water and sugar to a boil; continue to boil for 10 minutes. Remove from heat. Meanwhile, in a separate saucepan, bring remaining water to a boil; add teabags. Remove from heat and let steep for 20 minutes; discard bags. Add tea and concentrates to sugar water; stir in brandy. Pour into a freezer-safe container; freeze for at least 6 to 8 hours. To serve, fill a glass 2/3 full of slush; top with soda. Serves 20.

Leftover bits of fabric can find new life as beverage charms.
Trim fabric to a 4 to 5-inch strip and tie onto
glass stems. Simply charming!

Festive Holiday
Fare

Vada's Christmas Eve Wassail

Rhonda Lawson
Middletown, IN

Our family always gathered at my Aunt Vada's for her annual Christmas Eve open house. Aunt Vada was a special lady with a big heart. Even though she lived on limited means, she always made sure each of her nieces & nephews received a special gift from her. Upon entering her home, the sweet aroma of wassail and holiday goodies would greet us. Now I carry on the tradition of serving her Christmas wassail.

2 qts. apple cider
64-oz. can pineapple juice
2 c. orange juice
1 c. lemon juice

3 4-inch cinnamon sticks
1 t. whole cloves
8-oz. pkg. red cinnamon candies

Combine all ingredients in a slow cooker. Cover and cook on high setting for 2 hours, or until heated through and candies are melted. Reduce setting to low. Before serving, strain out cloves. Serves 18 to 20.

Enjoy plump Christmas stockings all throughout the season! Just stuff empty stockings with tissue paper or bubble wrap, then nestle a tiny gift, candy cane and greenery into the top until the big day arrives.

Snowed-In Snack Mix

Meg Dickinson
Champaign, IL

The winter my husband and I got married, it snowed...and snowed... and snowed. Trapped at home, we were craving something sweet. I concocted this sweet & salty popcorn mix with what we had on hand.

12-oz. pkg. white chocolate
   chips
3-oz. pkg. whole almonds

6 c. plain popped popcorn
1/4 t. salt
1 c. chocolate-covered raisins

Place chocolate chips in a small microwave-safe bowl; microwave on high setting for about 2 minutes, or until melted. In a small dry skillet over medium heat, toast almonds until golden and aromatic. Transfer almonds and popcorn to a large heatproof bowl. Sprinkle with salt and raisins; mix well. Drizzle melted chocolate over top; mix well. Turn out onto a large sheet of wax paper; cool. Break apart; store in an airtight container. Makes 8 servings.

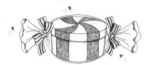

Eileen's Caramel Corn

Eileen Magiera
Milford, IN

Great recipe for those winter parties!

10 to 12 qts. popped popcorn
1/2 c. butter
14-oz. can sweetened condensed
   milk

1 c. light corn syrup
16-oz. pkg. powdered sugar
1 t. vanilla extract

Place popcorn in a very large heatproof bowl or kettle. In a saucepan, combine all ingredients except vanilla. Cook and stir over low heat for about 7 to 8 minutes, until mixture reaches the soft-ball stage, or 234 to 243 degrees on a candy thermometer. Stir in vanilla; immediately pour hot mixture over popcorn. Mix with a wooden spoon; cool before serving. Store in an airtight container. Makes 18 to 24 servings.

Festive Holiday Fare

Jack Frost's Snowflake Punch

Kristie Rigo
Friedens, PA

I like to invite friends over on a snowy evening to
play games and drink this punch. It's very, very good!

1/2 c. water
1 c. sugar
5-oz. can evaporated milk

3 2-ltr. bottles lemon-lime
soda, chilled
1/2 to 1 gal. vanilla ice cream

In a saucepan, combine water and sugar. Stir constantly over medium heat until sugar is dissolved. Remove from heat; stir in milk. Let cool. Chill mixture until ready to make punch. Right before serving, combine milk mixture and lemon-lime soda in a punch bowl. Add scoops of ice cream, adding more ice cream as desired. Serves 18 to 24.

Enjoying a fresh snowfall? Make Maple Snow Taffy! Heat one cup maple syrup and 1/4 cup butter until mixture reaches the thread stage, or 230 to 233 degrees on a candy thermometer. Let it cool for a few minutes, then pour it by the spoonful over bowls of clean snow. A wonderful New England wintertime treat!

Grinch Cocktail

Christina Addison
Clarksville, OH

This is a simple party punch recipe, yet guests will truly love it.
Since it's non-alcoholic, it's great for kids too!

1/3 c. sugar
6 T. plus 1-1/2 t. water
1/3 c. evaporated milk
Optional: 1/2 t. vanilla or
  almond extract

12 drops green food coloring
2-ltr. bottle lemon-lime soda,
  chilled
2 pts. vanilla ice cream

In a large saucepan, combine sugar and water. Cook and stir over medium heat until sugar is dissolved; remove from heat. Stir in milk and extract, if using. Transfer to a punch bowl; cover and refrigerate until chilled. Before serving, stir in food coloring and soda. Top with scoops of ice cream. Makes 4 quarts.

Make-Believe Champagne

Denise Piccirilli
Huber Heights, OH

This is so good and so easy to make. Even the "big kids" like it!

1-ltr. bottle carbonated water,
  chilled
1-ltr. bottle ginger ale, chilled

24-oz. bottle unsweetened white
  grape juice, chilled
ice cubes

In a large pitcher, combine bottled beverages; pour over ice cubes in chilled stemmed glasses. Makes 20 servings.

Keep an eye on yard sales for old serving trays. Découpage with Christmas cards or vintage postcards and top with a piece of glass. So handy for holiday entertaining!

Festive Holiday Fare

Spiced Chai Mix

Carmen Hyde
Spencerville, IN

*This sweet & spicy mix makes a wonderful drink for fall and winter.
It's also a great take-home favor for party guests.*

1 c. powdered non-fat milk
1 c. powdered non-dairy creamer
1 c. French vanilla-flavored
   powdered non-dairy creamer
2-1/2 c. sugar
1-1/2 c. unsweetened instant
   tea mix

1 t. ground ginger
1 t. cinnamon
1/2 t. ground cloves
1/2 t. cardamom
1/2 t. nutmeg
1/2 t. allspice
1/8 t. white pepper

Combine all ingredients in a large bowl; mix well. Blend in small
batches in a food processor until mixture is the consistency of fine
powder. Store in an airtight jar. To prepare, stir 4 heaping teaspoons
into a mug of hot milk. Makes 24 servings.

Candy Cane Cocoa

Jill Ball
Highland, UT

*Christmas Eve is a night of magic. We love to sit by the
Christmas tree in our new pajamas and drink hot cocoa.
This is a fun, festive twist on hot chocolate.*

4 c. milk
3 1-oz. sqs. semi-sweet baking
   chocolate, chopped
4 peppermint candy canes,
   crushed

Garnish: whipped cream, 4 mini
   peppermint candy canes

In a saucepan over medium-high heat, heat milk until hot, but not
boiling. Add chocolate and crushed peppermint; stir until melted and
smooth. Pour into 4 mugs; garnish with whipped cream. Serve each
with a candy cane stirring stick. Makes 4 servings.

After you write your annual holiday letter, be sure to save
a copy for yourself in a binder. You'll enjoy reading
past letters for years to come!

Christmas Yule Eggnog

Julie Stuart
Lockport, NY

This eggnog recipe is so yummy for the holidays. It's been in my husband's family for generations!

6 pasteurized eggs, separated
1/4 t. baking soda
2-1/4 c. sugar
Optional: 1/3 c. rum

2 c. milk
2 c. whipping cream
Garnish: nutmeg

With an electric mixer on medium speed, beat whites and yolks of eggs separately; transfer to a large bowl. Stir in baking soda, sugar and rum, if using. Beat mixture until stiff; add remaining ingredients. Stir well; cover and refrigerate overnight. Serve topped with nutmeg. Serves 6.

Eggless Eggnog

Abi Buening
Grand Forks, ND

The first time I made this recipe my hubby had no clue as to what was in the recipe. He thought it was real eggnog!

3-oz. pkg. instant French vanilla
    pudding mix
4 c. milk, divided
4 c. whipping cream

1/2 c. sugar
2 to 4 t. vanilla extract
Garnish: whipped topping,
    nutmeg

In a large bowl, stir together dry pudding mix and one cup of milk. When mixture begins to thicken, add remaining ingredients except garnish; mix well. Cover and chill. Garnish individual servings with whipped topping and a sprinkle of nutmeg. Makes 1/2 gallon.

Got leftover eggnog? Use it to make French toast the next morning... simply scrumptious!

Old-Fashioned Sugar Cookies

Kris Kellis
Salisbury, NC

This is an old, old recipe handed down in my twin sister's husband's family for generations. This is the perfect cookie dough for making Christmas cookies for Santa.

1/3 c. butter, softened
1/3 c. shortening
1 c. all-purpose flour
3/4 c. sugar
1 egg, beaten

1 T. milk
1 t. baking powder
1 t. vanilla extract
1/8 t. salt

In a large bowl, beat butter and shortening with an electric mixer on medium speed for 30 seconds. Add remaining ingredients; mix well. Cover and chill dough for 3 hours. On a lightly floured surface, roll out dough to a 1/8-inch thickness; cut into desired shapes with cookie cutters. Arrange on ungreased baking sheets. Bake at 375 degrees for 7 minutes, or until golden. Makes 2 dozen.

If you don't have plastic bubble wrap handy when you're packing cookies to mail, fill a few plastic zipping bags with just enough air to provide a little cushion. Nestle your cookies between air-filled bags...they'll arrive in perfect shape!

Sweet Treats to ❦ **Share** ❦

Frosted Walnut Cookies

Barbara Bower
Orrville, OH

We could not get through a family holiday gathering without this cookie on the table. It's a favorite any time of the year.

1/2 c. butter, softened	2 c. all-purpose flour
1-1/2 c. brown sugar, packed and divided	1/2 t. baking soda
	1/4 t. salt
1 egg, beaten	1/4 c. sour cream
1 t. vanilla extract	1 c. chopped walnuts

In a large bowl, beat butter and one cup brown sugar. Beat in egg and vanilla. In a separate bowl, mix flour, baking soda and salt; add to butter mixture, mixing well. Roll dough into walnut-size balls; place on ungreased baking sheets. Make a thumbprint in each ball. In a separate bowl, mix remaining brown sugar, sour cream and walnuts. Fill each thumbprint with a small spoonful of brown sugar mixture. Bake at 350 degrees for 8 to 10 minutes. Store in an airtight container or freeze. Makes 4 dozen.

Here's a handy kitchen tip! When measuring shortening, use a measuring cup larger than the portion needed. For example, if you need to measure 1/3 cup of shortening, use a one-cup measuring cup. Add 2/3 cup cold water and then add shortening until water fills the cup. No worries about air pockets leading to inaccurate measuring!

Grusti

Bethi Hendrickson
Danville, PA

My noni used to make these when I was a child. The box arrived at our house the week before Thanksgiving and Mom always hid it on the attic steps. They would get crispier as the days passed. My brother and I would sneak a taste at least once a day. My daddy would also make a few trips up those attic steps. When my mom started filling her tins for presents, we would hear her exclaiming about how half the box was gone. Of course she would look right at my brother and me, but my daddy would always take the full blame. Thanks, Daddy!

3/4 c. margarine, softened
5 c. sugar, divided
6 eggs, beaten
2 c. milk
1/4 c. whiskey

12 to 18 c. all-purpose flour
2 T. baking powder
1 t. salt
1/2 gal. oil for deep frying

In a large bowl, beat margarine, 2 cups sugar, eggs, milk and whiskey. In a separate bowl, combine 6 cups flour, baking powder and salt. Add flour mixture to margarine mixture; mix well. Blend in remaining flour, a cup at a time, until a stiff dough forms. Divide dough into small batches; roll out thinly on a floured surface. Cut dough into diamond shapes using a sharp knife or a cookie cutter. After all dough is cut, heat oil in a deep fryer or deep skillet. Fry cookies, a few at a time, in hot oil. Cook just until dough puffs; flip once. Immediately remove from oil; drain on paper towels. While still hot, shake cookies in a paper bag with one cup sugar; cool on wire racks. When the sugar gets lumpy, replace with another bag filled with one cup sugar. Store in a cardboard box lined with wax paper. Do not store in an airtight container, as cookies will get very crumbly. Makes about 8 dozen.

If you don't have a kitchen thermometer, here's a trick to tell when when your oil is hot enough to deep-fry in. Drop a popcorn kernel in the oil as it heats. The popcorn will pop when the oil is between 350 and 365 degrees, the perfect temperature for deep frying.

Sweet Treats to
❦ Share ❦

Doretha's Hedgehogs

Angie Stone
Argillite, KY

*A wonderful recipe that a sweet friend was generous enough
to share. All I can say is...delicious!*

1 c. chopped dates
2 c. walnuts, ground
2 c. sweetened flaked coconut,
   divided

1 c. brown sugar, packed
2 eggs, beaten

In a bowl, combine dates, walnuts, 1-1/2 cups coconut, brown sugar
and eggs. Roll dough into small balls. Roll each ball in remaining
coconut. Place on parchment paper-lined baking sheets; bake at
350 degrees for 10 to 12 minutes. Makes 3 dozen.

Apricot-Coconut Bites

Peggy Cadwell
Muncie, IN

*I spend whole evenings curled up by the fireplace reading **Gooseberry
Patch** cookbooks cover to cover. I've never sent a recipe before, but
want to share this favorite no-bake Christmas cookie. They are
melt-in-your-mouth wonderful!*

1-1/2 c. dried apricots, very
   finely chopped
2-1/4 c. sweetened flaked
   coconut

1/4 c. powdered sugar
2/3 c. sweetened condensed
   milk
1/3 c. sugar

In a bowl, combine all ingredients except sugar. Form mixture into
small balls, about 30 total. Roll in sugar. Store in an airtight container.
Flavor is better after 2 to 3 days; cookies keep for at least 2 weeks.
Makes about 2-1/2 dozen.

It is Christmas in the heart that puts
Christmas in the air.

–W.T. Ellis

Holiday Treasure Cookies

Candace Whitelock
Seaford, DE

This is a great recipe for getting children in the kitchen and excited about baking.

1-1/2 c. graham cracker crumbs
1/2 t. all-purpose flour
2 t. baking powder
14-oz. can sweetened condensed
    milk
1/2 c. butter, softened
1 c. pecans or walnuts, chopped

10-oz. pkg. mini milk chocolate
    drops
1-1/3 c. red, white and green
    candy-coated chocolates
1-1/3 c. sweetened flaked
    coconut

In a small bowl, stir together cracker crumbs, flour and baking powder; set aside. In a separate bowl, combine condensed milk and butter; beat until smooth. Add cracker crumb mixture; mix well. Stir in remaining ingredients. Drop by rounded tablespoonfuls onto ungreased baking sheets. Bake at 375 degrees for 8 to 10 minutes, until lightly golden. Cool on sheets one minute; remove to wire racks. Makes 3 dozen.

My first holiday memory is of making Christmas wreath cookies around the kitchen table with my mother and my aunt. We used corn flake cereal, marshmallows and green food coloring for the wreaths and red cinnamon candies and red licorice whips for the bows and berries. We baked many kinds of cookies, but these wreaths are what I remember best! It was the first of many times I can remember baking with my family for Christmas.

–Nancy Storms, Garfield, NJ

Sweet Treats to ☘ Share ☘

Candied Fruit Cookies

Patricia Brown
Ewing, VA

My mother always made these cookies at Christmas. I knew when we saw the candied fruit in the grocery store that it would soon be Christmas. I always looked forward to delivering these special cookies studded with red and green cherries to the neighbors.

1 c. shortening
2 c. brown sugar, packed
2 eggs, beaten
1/2 c. buttermilk
3-1/2 c. all-purpose flour
1 t. baking soda

1 t. salt
1-1/2 c. pecans, coarsely
   chopped
2 c. candied cherries, cut in half
2 c. chopped dates

In a large bowl, combine shortening, brown sugar and eggs. Stir in buttermilk. In a separate bowl, sift together flour, baking soda and salt. Stir flour mixture into shortening mixture; blend well. Stir in remaining ingredients. Chill dough for at least one hour. Drop by rounded teaspoonfuls, about 2 inches apart, onto lightly greased baking sheets. Bake at 400 degrees for 8 to 10 minutes, until almost no imprint remains when cookie is touched lightly. Makes 6 dozen.

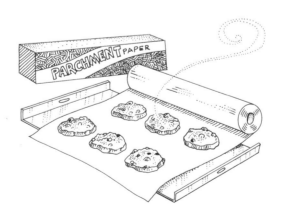

Generally, you can reuse parchment paper at least a few times when baking cookies. When it starts to darken and dry out, toss it.

Fudgy Brownie Cookies

Cynthia Dodge
Layton, UT

This cookie recipe is the most-requested recipe I have...they taste like soft, chocolatey brownies. Yum!

1/2 c. margarine, softened
1 c. sugar
1 egg, beaten
1/2 c. baking cocoa
2 T. oil

1-3/4 c. all-purpose flour
1/2 t. baking soda
1/2 t. salt
1/2 c. milk
2 t. vanilla extract

In a large bowl, beat margarine and sugar until fluffy. Add egg; beat well. In a separate bowl, mix cocoa and oil. Add to margarine mixture; blend well. In a separate bowl, combine flour, baking soda and salt. Add alternately with milk to margarine mixture. Add vanilla; stir well. Drop dough by rounded teaspoonfuls onto ungreased baking sheets. Bake at 375 degrees for 8 to 10 minutes. Cool on wire racks. Frost with Fudgy Chocolate Frosting. Store in a single layer in an airtight container; keep refrigerated. Makes 3 to 4 dozen.

Fudgy Chocolate Frosting:

3 T. baking cocoa
1 T. oil
1 c. powdered sugar

1/2 t. vanilla extract
1 to 1-1/2 T. milk

In a bowl, mix cocoa and oil until well blended. Stir in sugar and vanilla. Gradually add milk; beat with an electric mixer on medium speed until smooth.

Make adorable mini treat baskets from garden peat pots! Simply cut out clean peat pots to create individual baskets, and apply one to two coats of chalkboard paint. Let dry; punch holes in the sides to add a twine or ribbon handle. Tuck in a piece of tissue paper before filling with treats; use chalk to personalize.

Sweet Treats to
❦ Share ❧

Grandma's Vanilla Balls

Nicole Shira
New Baltimore, MI

This recipe was handed down to my sister-in-law by her grandmother. It's been in her family for more than one hundred years. I triple this recipe and the cookies still disappear in days.

3/4 c. butter, softened
1/4 c. sweetened condensed
  milk
1 t. vanilla extract
1-3/4 c. all-purpose flour

6 T. powdered sugar
1 c. chopped pecans
Garnish: additional powdered
  sugar

In a large bowl, combine all ingredients except garnish; mix well. Roll into walnut-sized balls. Place on ungreased baking sheets. Bake at 325 degrees for 15 minutes. Allow to cool slightly. While still warm, roll balls in additional powdered sugar. Makes about 2 dozen.

Chocolate Peppermint Cookies

Kris Warner
Circleville, OH

My kids and I make these cookies every Christmas. Set a couple aside for Santa, because they go fast!

18-1/4 oz. pkg. devil's food
  cake mix
1/2 c. butter, softened
1 T. water

2 eggs, beaten
2 T. powdered sugar
2 5.3-oz. pkgs. mini chocolate-
  covered mint patties

In a large bowl, combine dry cake mix, butter and water. Add eggs; mix well. Shape dough into one-inch balls; roll in powdered sugar. Place 2 inches apart on ungreased baking sheets. Bake at 375 degrees for 8 minutes. Remove from oven; immediately press a mint patty into each cookie. Makes 2 dozen.

Give a giant peppermint stick filled with Chocolate Peppermint Cookies! Stack cookies in a clear plastic mailing tube with red craft tape spiraled around it.

Pistachio Wreath Cookies

Natasha Spillett
Alberta, Canada

My family loves this recipe! We make it every year and I always have to make at least two batches because the first one gets eaten right away. For the best possible cookies, don't let the dough get too warm when you're rolling it into ropes.

2 c. all-purpose flour
1/4 t. baking powder
1/4 t. salt
3/4 c. butter
3/4 c. sugar
1 egg, beaten

1/2 t. vanilla extract
1/2 t. almond extract
1/4 c. pistachios, coarsely
    chopped
1/4 t. green food coloring

In a large bowl, combine flour, baking powder and salt. In a separate bowl, beat butter until softened; add sugar and beat until fluffy. Add egg, extracts and pistachios. Add butter mixture to flour mixture; mix well. Divide dough in half. Add green food coloring to one half; mix well. Keeping dough separate, wrap in plastic wrap and chill for at least 30 minutes. On a lightly floured surface, roll about a tablespoon of plain dough into a 6-inch rope. Repeat with green dough. Place ropes side-by-side and twist together 6 times. Shape twisted dough in a circle; gently pinch ends together. Place on an ungreased baking sheet. Repeat steps until no dough remains. Bake at 375 degrees for 10 minutes. Cool on wire racks. Makes 12 to 15 cookies.

One of my favorite traditions is baking Christmas cookies with my family. I've been doing it since my husband and I were dating, almost 30 years ago! Since the temperature on my parents' oven wasn't working properly, we baked dozens and dozens of cookies in a tiny toaster oven, six at a time. Now, I have three daughters who continue the tradition of baking and giving cookies...we spend days mixing, baking and eating many of the same cookies that my husband and I baked all those years ago.

–Cindy Fitzpatrick, Arnold, MD

Sweet Treats to
❦ Share ❧

Cobblestone Cookies

Brenda Huey
Geneva, IN

I received this excellent cookie recipe from a friend. They've since become the signature cookie of my bakery, the Cobblestone Bakery in Berne, Indiana. It is such a tasty and different cookie!

1-1/2 c. shortening
1/4 c. milk
3 c. sugar
1-1/2 c. cream cheese, softened

1 t. vanilla extract
3-1/2 c. all-purpose flour
1 c. chopped pecans

In a large bowl with an electric mixer on medium speed, combine shortening, milk, sugar, cream cheese and vanilla. Add flour and pecans. Drop by rounded teaspoonfuls onto ungreased baking sheets. Bake at 325 degrees for 18 to 20 minutes. Cool on wire racks; frost with Cobblestone Frosting. Makes 3 dozen.

Cobblestone Frosting:

1/2 c. shortening
2 c. powdered sugar
1/2 t. salt

1/4 c. milk
1/2 t. almond extract

In a bowl, combine all ingredients; mix well.

Enjoy fresh-baked cookies in minutes by freezing some of your cookie dough! Simply drop rounded spoonfuls on a parchment-lined baking sheet, freeze until firm and transfer to a plastic zipping bag. When you're ready to bake, just add a few extra minutes of baking time.

Aunt Barbara's Gingerbread Men

Barbara Hanson
Kimberly, WI

I don't dare show up at a family Christmas gathering without my famous gingerbread men! The butterscotch glaze has a hint of orange flavoring that makes this recipe unique. For a festive look, dip the hands, feet and top of the heads in melted white chocolate.

1/4 c. boiling water	1/2 c. brown sugar, packed
1/2 c. butter, softened	1/2 c. light molasses
1-1/2 t. ground ginger	3 c. all-purpose flour
1/2 t. nutmeg	1/2 t. baking soda
1/8 t. ground cloves	1 t. salt

In a large bowl, pour boiling water over butter. Add spices, brown sugar and molasses; mix until well blended. Beat in flour; chill dough thoroughly. Roll dough out on a floured surface to a 1/4-inch thickness. Cut with cookie cutters; place on ungreased baking sheets. Bake at 375 degrees for 10 to 12 minutes. Cool completely. Frost with Butterscotch Orange Glaze or your favorite frosting. Makes 2 to 4 dozen.

Butterscotch Orange Glaze:

2 c. butterscotch chips, divided   1/2 t. orange extract, divided
3 t. oil, divided

In a microwave-safe bowl, combine one cup chips, 1-1/2 teaspoons oil and 1/4 teaspoon extract. Microwave on high setting until chips are melted, checking at one-minute intervals. Stir well; dip cookies in glaze. Place on wax paper; let cool. Repeat steps for remaining ingredients, until all cookies are dipped.

No time to frost your gingerbread? Just top with a stencil and gently dust with powdered sugar or glittery sanding sugar...beautiful!

Sweet Treats to
🍃 Share 🍃

Coconut-Cranberry Bars

Jeannie Wolf
Findlay, OH

I made this recipe for our county fair and won First Place in the bar cookie category, then Best of Show for all cookies!

1-1/2 c. plus 1/3 c. all-purpose
  flour, divided
3/4 c. sugar
3/4 c. chilled butter
2 c. sweetened flaked coconut
1 c. sweetened dried cranberries

3/4 c. chopped walnuts
3/4 c. brown sugar, packed
3 eggs, beaten
1-1/2 t. vanilla extract
1/4 t. salt

In a large bowl, combine 1-1/2 cups flour and sugar; cut in butter with a pastry blender or fork until mixture resembles coarse crumbs. Press mixture into an ungreased 13"x9" baking pan. Bake at 350 degrees for 15 minutes, or until edges are lightly golden. Remove from oven. Combine all remaining ingredients; mix well. Spread over warm crust in pan. Bake for 20 to 25 minutes longer, until golden. Cool completely; cut into bars. Makes about 20.

To freshen up last year's artificial flower bouquets, place the flowers in a plastic bag, pour in a few teaspoons of salt and shake. The salt helps to remove any dust and dirt!

Holiday Strawberry Bars

Dorothy Kast
San Jose, CA

This is one of my most-requested recipes!

1 c. butter, softened
1 c. sugar
2 egg yolks, beaten

2 c. all-purpose flour
1 c. chopped walnuts
1/2 c. strawberry jam

In a bowl, beat butter until fluffy; add sugar and egg yolks. Blend in flour and walnuts. Press half the dough into a greased 8"x8" baking pan. Spread jam over top, keeping jam about 1/2 inch from edge of pan. Add remaining dough, spreading it over top of jam layer. Press dough down with floured hands. Bake at 325 degrees for one hour. Cool; cut into squares. Makes about 2 dozen.

Kipplens

Susan Bohannon
Spring Hill, TN

My Great-Aunt Hilda used to make these cookies during the holidays and my brothers, cousins and I would practically eat them all. They're so delicious! We have passed this recipe down through the generations and now my daughters bake them as well.

2 c. butter, softened
1 c. sugar
1/4 t. salt
5 c. all-purpose flour

2 t. vanilla extract
2 c. chopped pecans
Garnish: powdered sugar,
   additional sugar

In a large bowl, beat butter until fluffy; add remaining ingredients except garnish in order given. Dough will be very stiff. Pinch and roll dough into walnut-size balls. Place on ungreased baking sheets, about one inch apart. Bake at 325 degrees for 28 minutes. While still warm, roll each cookie first in powdered sugar, then in granulated sugar until coated on all sides. Makes 2 dozen.

Sweet Treats to
❦ **Share** ❧

Butterscotch Apple Blondies

Jackie Smulski
Lyons, IL

One of my favorite treats! You can also try peanut butter chips instead of butterscotch. Both are incredibly wonderful.

2 c. sugar
2 eggs, beaten
3/4 c. oil
2-1/2 c. self-rising flour
1 t. cinnamon

1/8 t. nutmeg
3 c. tart apples, cored, peeled
    and diced
1 c. finely chopped walnuts
2/3 c. butterscotch chips

In a bowl, combine sugar, eggs and oil; mix well. Stir in flour, cinnamon and nutmeg. Batter will be thick. Fold in apples and walnuts. Spread into a greased 13"x9" baking pan. Sprinkle butterscotch chips over top. Bake at 350 degrees for 35 to 40 minutes, until golden and a toothpick inserted in the center comes out clean. Cool; cut into squares. Makes 2 dozen.

Make plain cupcakes special with two-tone frosting! Fill two decorating bags with the colors you'll be using; do not add a tip. Twist the tops of the bags and cut off about 1/2 inch from the ends of each filled bag. Take a third, empty bag; snip the end off and add your favorite piping tip. Now, load the filled frosting bags inside the bag with the piping tip. Twist the top of the bag and pipe as usual.

193

Triple-Chocolate Coffee Brownies

Dawn Romero
Lewisville, TX

A wonderful treat for anyone who loves coffee, brownies and extra chocolate!

1 egg, beaten
1/4 c. oil
1/4 c. strong brewed coffee,
  slightly cooled
1/4 c. water
21-oz. pkg. fudge brownie mix

3/4 c. milk chocolate chips
3/4 c. white chocolate chips
1/2 c. semi-sweet chocolate
  chips
1/2 c. chopped pecans or
  walnuts

In a large bowl, mix egg, oil, coffee and water. Add dry brownie mix; mix well. Fold in chocolate chips and nuts. Spread into a greased 13"x9" baking pan. Bake at 350 degrees for 30 minutes. Cool; cut into bars or squares. Serves 8 to 10.

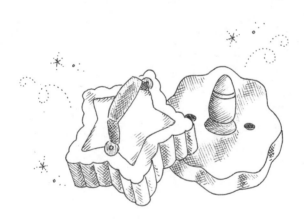

To cut your brownies into fun holiday shapes, line the pan with aluminum foil before pouring in batter. Once brownies are cooled to room temperature, refrigerate until firm. Remove brownies from pan by lifting up on the foil. Peel foil down from the sides. Using a cookie cutter, cut brownies as close together as possible; gently push the top of the brownie to remove from the cutter.

Sweet Treats to Share

Sour Cream Raisin Squares

Lori Peterson
Effingham, KS

A friend of my grandmother's at the nursing home shared this delicious recipe with us along with a sample. It's oh-so good!

1 c. butter, softened
1 c. brown sugar, packed
2 c. all-purpose flour
2 c. quick-cooking oats,
   uncooked
1 t. baking soda
1 t. baking powder

1/8 t. salt
1-1/2 T. cornstarch
1 c. sugar
4 egg yolks
1-1/2 c. raisins
2 c. sour cream

In a bowl, beat butter and sugar. Add flour, oats, baking soda, baking powder and salt; mix until crumbly. Reserve 2 cups of oat mixture. Press remaining oat mixture into a lightly greased 13"x9" baking pan. Bake at 350 degrees for 15 minutes. Remove from oven; cool. In a saucepan, combine remaining ingredients. Bring to a boil and cook over high heat, stirring often, for 8 minutes. Pour over baked crust. Sprinkle with remaining oat mixture. Bake for 15 minutes longer, or until golden. Cool; cut into squares. Makes 15 to 20.

Winter is prime bird-feeding season, but commercial birdseed mixes tend to be expensive. Mix up your own special blend by buying peanuts, sunflower seeds and cracked corn in bulk.

Orange Swirl Fudge

Karen Hood Keeney
Bronston, KY

I have my own sweet shop, Karen's Konfections, and I love to try new recipes. One day my brother Terry came to me with this recipe and asked me if I could make it for him. It's a winner!

3 c. sugar
2/3 c. whipping cream
3/4 c. butter
11-oz. pkg. white chocolate
   chips

7-oz. jar marshmallow creme
12 drops yellow food coloring
9 drops red food coloring
1 T. orange extract

In a large saucepan over medium heat, combine sugar, cream and butter. Stir mixture until it reaches the soft-ball stage, or 234 to 243 degrees on a candy thermometer. Remove from heat. Add chocolate chips and marshmallow creme; stir until melted and smooth. Reserve one cup fudge; to the remaining fudge add food coloring and extract, mixing well. Pour into a buttered 13"x9" baking pan. Spoon reserved fudge over top; swirl with a table knife. Cool; cut into squares. Makes about 3 dozen.

Fudge keeps well and makes a wonderful gift! Since it isn't prone to crumbling, it's a perfect choice for mailing to loved ones in faraway places. Wrap tightly in plastic wrap before boxing it up.

Jingle Bell Fudge

Julie Guntzel
Bemidji, MN

I came up with this recipe to add something new and different to my Christmas baking.

3/4 c. butter, softened
3 c. sugar
5-oz. can evaporated milk
12-oz. pkg. white chocolate
    chips

7-oz. jar marshmallow creme
1 t. vanilla extract
1-1/2 t. cinnamon extract
10 to 15 drops red food coloring

In a saucepan, combine butter, sugar and evaporated milk. Cook and stir over low heat until sugar is dissolved. Bring to a boil over medium heat; boil mixture for 4 minutes, stirring occasionally. Remove from heat. Stir in chips, marshmallow creme and vanilla until smooth. Reserve one cup of fudge; to this, add cinnamon extract and desired amount of red food coloring. Pour remaining untinted fudge into a 13"x9" baking pan lined with aluminum foil and generously buttered. Spoon red-tinted fudge on top; swirl with a table knife. Cool completely. Using foil, lift fudge out of pan. Cut into one-inch squares. Store in an airtight container. Makes about 8 dozen.

Always make candy just one batch at a time. Don't be tempted to double or triple the recipe, because the candy may fail to set up properly.

Coffee Cream Fudge

Janis Parr
Ontario, Canada

If you are a coffee lover, you will love this rich, creamy fudge.

2 c. brown sugar, packed
1/2 c. strong brewed coffee,
   chilled
1/4 c. whipping cream

2 T. butter
1/8 t. salt
1/2 c. chopped pecans
   or walnuts

In a saucepan over low heat, combine sugar, coffee and cream. Bring mixture to a slow boil without stirring; then cook and stir mixture until it reaches the soft-ball stage, or 234 to 243 degrees on a candy thermometer. Remove from heat. Stir in butter and salt; cool. Beat for several minutes, until fudge has thickened and gloss is almost gone. Fold in nuts. Pour into a buttered 8"x8" baking pan. Cool; cut into squares. Makes 2 dozen.

Key Lime Fudge

Machelle Anderson
Central City, NE

My family loves this refreshing alternative to traditional fudge.
The best part is, it's so easy to make!

3 c. white chocolate chips
14-oz. can sweetened condensed
   milk
2 t. Key lime zest
2 T. Key lime juice

1 c. chopped macadamia nuts,
   toasted
Optional: coarsely chopped
   macadamia nuts, sweetened
   flaked coconut

In a saucepan over low heat, melt chocolate chips and condensed milk; stir until smooth. Remove from heat; stir in zest and juice. Fold in nuts. Spread mixture in an 8"x8" baking pan lined with aluminum foil and generously buttered. If desired, sprinkle with additional nuts and coconut. Cover and chill for at least 2 hours. Lift fudge out of pan; cut into squares. Store in an airtight container at room temperature. Makes 2-1/2 pounds.

Sweet Treats to
❧ Share ☙

Peppermint Hearts

Tina Butler
Royse City, TX

Share a little love this Christmas with Peppermint Hearts.
These little hearts look so cute in festive tissue paper-lined
holiday tins or clear gift bags.

64 mini peppermint candy
  canes, unwrapped
3/4 lb. white or semi-sweet
  melting chocolate

Optional: additional peppermint
  candy canes, crushed

Line a baking sheet with wax paper. Arrange candy canes on baking sheet in groups of 2 to form heart shapes. Place melting chocolate in a microwave-safe bowl. Microwave on the defrost setting, 3 minutes at a time, stirring after each interval, until chocolate is melted, about 5 to 6 minutes. Spoon or pipe melted chocolate into centers of hearts until all the open space is filled. Sprinkle with crushed candy canes, if using. Allow to harden; store in airtight containers. Makes 2-1/2 dozen.

Create a sweet goodie bag from a plain paper sack!
Fold the top over, punch two holes and slide a
peppermint stick through.

199

Peanut Patties

Cathy Callen
Lawton, OK

I use muffin tins, sprayed with non-stick spray, to make my peanut patties. They make a very neat patty!

2-1/2 c. sugar
2/3 c. corn syrup
1 c. evaporated milk
3 c. raw peanuts

1 t. butter
1 t. vanilla extract
2 to 3 drops red food coloring

In a saucepan, mix sugar, corn syrup, milk and peanuts; cook over medium heat until mixture starts to boil. Reduce heat to very low; continue to cook for one hour, stirring occasionally. Remove from heat; stir in remaining ingredients. Beat mixture until thick and creamy. Pour into greased muffin cups; cool. Makes 2 dozen.

Angel Clouds

Andrea Heyart
Aubrey, TX

Many years ago, when I first moved out of my parents' house and into my own place, I raided my mother's recipe box. I copied not only my favorite recipes but also some that had never seen the light of day, yet sounded interesting. For some reason this delicious concoction fell into the later category. They are now a favorite!

11-oz. pkg. white chocolate
   chips
16-oz. can creamy vanilla
   frosting

36 marshmallows
3 to 4 T. candy sprinkles

In a saucepan over low heat, combine chips and frosting; stir until smooth. Pour half the mixture into a 9"x9" baking pan lined with aluminum foil. Arrange marshmallows over top in a single layer. Pour remaining chocolate mixture over top. Sprinkle with candy sprinkles. Refrigerate for 2 hours. Remove from pan by lifting foil; cut into squares. Makes one dozen.

Sweet Treats to Share

New Year's Nut Roll

Linda Richardson
Brunswick, OH

*You won't believe how good this is! After my mom made it
one year, I had to have it for every New Year's Day.*

16-oz. pkg. graham crackers,
    crushed and divided
16-oz. pkg. pitted whole dates,
    finely chopped
16-oz. pkg. marshmallows,
    finely chopped

14-1/2 oz. jar maraschino
    cherries, drained
16 English walnuts, shelled and
    finely chopped
1 c. whipping cream

Set aside 3/4 cup crushed graham crackers; place the rest in a large
bowl. To bowl, add dates, marshmallows, cherries, walnuts and just
enough cream to moisten and hold mixture together. Turn mixture out
onto wax paper; roll into a log about 12 inches long. Roll in reserved
cracker crumbs. Wrap in wax paper; chill. Before serving, whip
remaining cream. Slice nut roll into 3/4-inch slices; top with whipped
cream. Serves 16.

When I was a little girl I had an Aunt Jane who lived with my
grandmother. My aunt did not work, therefore she had no money
to spend on Christmas gifts, but she sure could make great
cookies, many kinds and shapes. Every Christmas she would bake
a shoebox full of cookies for my brother and me. Wrapped in
festive paper with a bow, this was her present to us and we loved
getting this wonderful box of cookies from our loving Aunt Jane.
I like to imagine her in heaven now, still baking cookies and
putting them into a shoebox.

–Carol Riddle, Bluefield, WV

Chocolate Red Wine Cupcakes
Donna Nowicki
Center City, MN

I teach a gourmet cupcake baking class at a local cooking school. This recipe is one of the most popular in the class. My son, who is a professional chef, said these were the best cupcakes he's ever tasted!

3/4 c. semi-sweet chocolate
   chips
1/2 c. baking cocoa
1/2 c. boiling water
1 c. butter, softened
1-1/2 c. sugar
4 eggs

1-1/4 c. all-purpose flour
1-1/2 t. baking powder
1 t. salt
3/4 c. Italian sparkling red wine
Garnish: red sugar, dark
   chocolate drops

In a bowl, combine chocolate chips and cocoa. Pour boiling water over top and whisk until chocolate is melted. In a large bowl, beat butter and sugar until fluffy. Beat in eggs, one at a time. In a separate bowl, combine flour, baking powder and salt. Slowly add to butter mixture; mix well. Alternately add chocolate mixture and wine to butter mixture; blend well. Pour batter into paper-lined muffin cups, filling cups 2/3 full. Bake at 350 degrees for 20 minutes, or until a toothpick inserted in the center comes out clean. Cool. Frost with White Chocolate Buttercream Frosting. Garnish with a sprinkling of red sugar and a chocolate drop. Makes 18.

White Chocolate Buttercream Frosting:

5 1-oz. sqs. white baking
   chocolate, chopped
3/4 c. cream cheese, softened
1/4 c. butter, softened

1/8 t. salt
1 t. vanilla extract
2-1/2 c. powdered sugar,
   divided

Melt chocolate in a double boiler. Remove from heat; set aside until lukewarm. In a large bowl with an electric mixer on medium speed, beat cream cheese and butter until smooth. Add chocolate, salt and vanilla; mix well. Add 2 cups powdered sugar; beat on high speed for 3 minutes. If mixture is too thin, add remaining powdered sugar; beat on high speed for 7 minutes more.

Sweet Treats to
❧ Share ❧

Peppermint Marble Cake

*Arlenna Martinez
Long Beach, CA*

*This may seem like a long, complicated recipe, but it looks
so grand and tastes amazing. If you want a show-stopping
holiday dessert, this three-layer cake is it!*

18-1/4 oz. pkg. white cake mix
3 egg whites, beaten
1-1/3 c. plus 1/2 c. buttermilk
2 T. oil
9-oz. pkg. yellow cake mix

1 egg, beaten
1-1/2 T. baking cocoa
1/2 t. baking soda
2 T. red food coloring
1 t. cider vinegar

In a large bowl, combine dry white cake mix, egg whites, 1-1/3 cups
buttermilk and oil. With an electric mixer on medium speed, beat until
well blended. In a separate large bowl, combine dry yellow cake mix
and remaining ingredients. Beat with an electric mixer on medium
speed until well blended. Alternately spoon cake batters into 3 greased
and floured 9" round cake pans; swirl colors together with a table
knife. Bake at 350 degrees for 22 to 25 minutes, until a wooden
toothpick inserted in center comes out clean. Cool in pans on wire
racks for 10 minutes. Frost with Peppermint Cream Cheese Frosting
between layers and over top and sides of cake. Serve immediately;
refrigerate leftovers. Serves 10 to 12.

Peppermint Cream Cheese Frosting:

8-oz. pkg. cream cheese,
    softened
1 c. butter, softened

2 t. peppermint extract
32-oz. pkg. powdered sugar

In a bowl with an electric mixer on medium speed, beat cream cheese
and butter until fluffy. Add extract; lower speed and add powdered
sugar a little at a time until well blended.

Pumpkin-Pecan Rum Cake

Shirley Harris
Fairview, TX

This is a a wonderful buffet cake...it always disappears quickly!

3/4 c. chopped pecans
3 c. all-purpose flour
2 T. pumpkin pie spice
2 t. baking soda
1 t. salt
1 c. butter, softened

1 c. brown sugar, packed
1 c. sugar
4 eggs
15-oz. can pumpkin
1 t. vanilla extract

Grease a Bundt® pan; sprinkle nuts in bottom. In a bowl, mix flour, pumpkin pie spice, baking soda and salt. In a separate large bowl, beat butter and sugars until fluffy. Add eggs, one at a time, beating well after each addition. Add pumpkin and vanilla; mix well. Add flour mixture to butter mixture, 1/3 at a time, mixing well after each addition. Spoon batter into pan. Bake at 325 degrees for 60 to 70 minutes, until a wooden pick inserted into cake comes out clean. Cool 10 minutes. Poke holes in cake with a long pick; pour half of Rum Butter Glaze over top. Let stand 5 minutes; invert onto a serving plate. Poke more holes in top of cake; pour remaining glaze over cake. Let cool. Serves 12.

Rum Butter Glaze:

1/2 c. butter
1 c. sugar
1/4 c. water

5 to 6 T. dark rum, or
1-1/2 to 2 t. rum extract

In a saucepan over medium heat, melt butter. Stir in sugar and water; bring to a boil. Remove from heat. Stir in rum or extract.

To neatly glaze a cake, cut five strips of wax paper into 4-inch lengths and slide under the cake on all sides of the cake server. Glaze cake as instructed. Leave wax paper strips in place until the glaze sets. Carefully remove strips before serving...no mess!

Glazed Devil's Food Cake

Judy Yeager
Frankfort, KY

This cake is a favorite of my family. I make it whenever we get together for special occasions, and it doesn't last long.

18-1/4 oz. pkg. devil's food cake
   mix with pudding
1 c. sour cream
4 eggs, beaten

1/2 c. oil
1/2 c. water
2 c. semi-sweet chocolate chips
1 c. chopped walnuts

In a large bowl with an electric mixer on medium speed, beat dry cake mix, sour cream, eggs, oil and water. Fold in chocolate chips and nuts. Pour into a well-greased Bundt® pan. Bake at 350 degrees for 55 to 60 minutes, until a toothpick tests clean. Cool in pan for about 30 minutes. Pour Vanilla Glaze over top. Serves 12.

Vanilla Glaze:

1/2 c. brown sugar, packed
1/2 c. sugar
1/4 c. evaporated milk

1/4 c. butter
1/2 t. vanilla extract

In a saucepan over medium heat, combine all ingredients except vanilla; bring to a boil, stirring often. Boil for one minute; remove from heat. Stir in vanilla. Beat with an electric mixer on medium speed for about 8 minutes. If glaze gets too thick to pour, add a little more milk until the desired consistency is reached. Double glaze recipe if you want to cover the entire cake.

For ready-to-bake desserts at any time, make and freeze treats like cobblers and bread puddings in individual-sized ramekins. Perfectly portioned for pop-in guests!

Grandma Griffitts' Orange Slice Cake

Deana Osborne
Somerset, KY

When I was growing up, my family would go to Oklahoma for Christmas to see our grandparents and extended family. Each time we would go to my aunt's house and watch her make all the Christmas candies and pies. This makes a sweet, bread-like cake.

1/4 c. oil	3-1/2 c. all-purpose flour
1 c. butter	1/2 c. buttermilk
2 c. sugar	9-oz. pkg. orange slice candy,
4 eggs, beaten	chopped
1 t. baking soda	8-oz. pkg. chopped dates
2 c. chopped nuts	2 c. sweetened flaked coconut

In a bowl, combine all ingredients; mix well. Pour into 3 greased, 8"x4" loaf pans. Bake at 275 degrees for 1-1/2 hours. Makes 3 loaves.

Snowdrop Cookies

Joni Rick
Murrieta, CA

This is a wonderful shortcut recipe when I need a quick gift or treat to share. You can make many variations with this cookie dough...use any flavor cake mix and extracts and add your own fun touches!

18-1/2 oz. pkg. yellow or white cake mix	zest of 1 orange
	1 t. orange extract
2 eggs, beaten	1 c. sweetened dried cranberries
1/3 c. canola oil	1 c. chopped pecans or walnuts

In a large bowl, combine dry cake mix, eggs and oil; beat until well blended. Stir in remaining ingredients. Drop by rounded teaspoonfuls onto lightly greased baking sheets. Bake at 350 degrees for 10 to 12 minutes, until edges are lightly golden. Cool on wire racks. Makes 3 dozen.

Sweet Treats to
❧ Share ☙

Carol's Holiday Pound Cake

Carol McKeon
Lebanon, TN

Our family is not fond of traditional fruitcake, so some years ago, I created this pound cake version. Now it's a family favorite! My cousin Dolores says that when you slice it and freeze it, it takes like ice cream when you eat it. Yum!

8-oz. pkg. cream cheese, softened
1 c. butter, softened
1 c. sugar
1-1/2 t. vanilla extract
4 eggs
2-1/4 c. all-purpose flour, divided

1-1/2 t. baking powder
1/2 t. salt
14-1/2 oz. jar maraschino cherries, drained and liquid reserved

In a large bowl, beat cream cheese and butter until fluffy. Beat in sugar and vanilla. Add eggs, one at a time, beating well after each. In a separate bowl, blend together 2 cups flour, baking powder and salt. Add flour mixture to cream cheese mixture; blend well. Cut 10 to 12 cherries into quarters; toss with remaining flour. Add coated cherries to batter. Stir in 2 tablespoons reserved cherry liquid. Batter will be thick. Spoon into a greased and floured Bundt® pan. Bake for 75 minutes, or until cake tests done with a toothpick and cake springs back when lightly touched. Serves 8 to 10.

Turn a Bundt® cake into a holiday wreath. Drizzle with frosting, then sprinkle chopped green and red candied cherries over the top. Twist a long strip of red fruit leather into a jaunty bow to complete the wreath.

Tres Leches Cake

Tina Butler
Royse City, TX

One of my favorite cakes is Tres Leches Cake, meaning Three Milks Cake. This is a Mexican-inspired cake that is so yummy. You can serve this cake without the fruit topping, but if you have time it's worth the extra step. It looks so pretty!

18-1/4 oz. pkg. yellow cake mix
14-oz. can sweetened condensed
   milk
5-oz. can evaporated milk
7.6-oz. can media crema or
   1 c. whole milk

8-oz. container frozen whipped
   topping, thawed
Optional: sliced fruit, such as
   strawberries, pineapple
   chunks, mandarin oranges
   and kiwi

Prepare cake mix according to package directions; bake in a 13"x9" baking pan. While cake is still warm, pierce surface all over with a toothpick or wooden skewer, about every 1/2 inch. Combine milks; slowly and evenly pour over cake. The cake should absorb all of the liquid if it is poured slowly. Allow cake to stand at room temperature for 30 minutes. Cover with plastic wrap or aluminum foil; refrigerate for at least 30 minutes, until well chilled. Frost cake with whipped topping before serving and decorate with fruit, if using. Keep refrigerated. Cut into squares. Serves 8 to 10.

Here's a fun way to keep plastic wrap from sticking to frosting when you're transporting a dessert. Take a few toothpicks and stick mini marshmallow on the ends. Stick the other end of each toothpick into the cake. Gently cover with plastic wrap...the toothpicks won't poke holes through the wrap!

Sweet Treats to
☙ Share ❧

French Apple Cobbler

Cindy Beach
Franklin, NY

I received this recipe from a woman who lived across the hall from me when I was single and residing in my very first apartment, 25 years ago. It is one of my most-requested recipes.

7 to 8 apples, cored, peeled
   and sliced
3 c. sugar, divided
1-3/4 c. all-purpose flour
1 t. cinnamon
1-1/4 t. salt, divided

2 t. vanilla extract
1/2 c. butter, softened and
   divided
1-1/2 t. baking powder
3 eggs, beaten

In a large bowl, combine apples, 1-1/2 cups sugar, 1/4 cup flour, cinnamon, 1/2 teaspoon salt, vanilla and 2 tablespoons butter. Mix well. Spread in a well-greased 13"x9" baking pan. In a separate bowl, combine remaining ingredients; mix well. Pour over apple mixture in pan; do not stir. Bake at 350 degrees for 25 to 30 minutes, until golden. Serves 12 to 15.

Kids will love these sweet reindeer cookies! Start with your favorite plain drop cookie dough, like peanut butter or gingerbread. Shape into one-inch balls. Pinch one side of the ball to form a point and gently flatten with your hand. Bake as directed. Remove from oven; immediately press two mini pretzels into the tops of the cookies for the antlers, two mini brown candy-coated chocolates for the eyes and a regular-size red candy-coated chocolate for the nose.

Gingerbread Cheesecake

Amy Hunt
Traphill, NC

This cheesecake is a delicious addition to your Christmas table.

50 Moravian spice or molasses
    thin wafer cookies
1/2 c. butter, melted
3 eggs, beaten
3/4 c. sugar
8-oz. pkg. cream cheese,
    softened

1 T. orange zest
2 T. orange juice
1 c. sour cream
1/2 c. powdered sugar

Crush cookies into fine crumbs; set aside 3 tablespoons. In a bowl, combine remaining crumbs and butter. Press into a greased 8" springform pan. Bake at 350 degrees for 10 minutes. In a large bowl, combine eggs and sugar; mix well. Fold in cream cheese, zest and juice. Spread egg mixture over baked crust. Bake at 350 degrees for 30 minutes. Cool completely. In a bowl, combine sour cream and powdered sugar; spread over baked cake. Garnish with reserved cookie crumbs. Remove from springform pan before slicing. Serves 8 to 10.

Don't toss that lemon or orange half after it's been juiced!
Wrap it and store in the freezer, and it'll be ready to grate
whenever a recipe calls for fresh citrus zest.

Sweet Treats to
❦ Share ❧

Sticky Apple Pudding Cake

Andrea Vernon
Logansport, IN

This is a special recipe from my mom. I've never seen another recipe like it. The sauce is very sweet and a little goes a long way. Save any leftover sauce to serve with ice cream later...yum!

1 c. sugar	1/2 t. cinnamon
1/2 c. butter	1/2 t. nutmeg
1 egg, beaten	1/2 t. salt
1 t. vanilla extract	3 Granny Smith apples, cored,
1 c. all-purpose flour	peeled and grated
1 t. baking soda	1/2 c. toasted pecans or walnuts

In a bowl, beat sugar, butter, egg and vanilla until creamy. Stir in remaining ingredients. Pour into a greased 8"x8" or 9"x9" baking pan; bake at 350 degrees for 40 minutes, or until golden. Top individual servings with warm Caramel Sauce. Serves 6.

Caramel Sauce:

1/2 c. butter	2 t. vanilla extract
1 c. brown sugar, packed	1/2 t. salt
1 c. sugar	
14-oz. can sweetened condensed	
milk	

In a saucepan over medium heat, combine butter and sugars; cook and stir until sugars dissolve. Add condensed milk; bring to a boil. Remove from heat; stir in vanilla and salt. Cool slightly before serving. Refrigerate any leftover sauce in an airtight container.

Cutting a round cake? You'll get more pieces in less time with this method: Use a long, sharp knife to cut a smaller circle inside the larger one. Cut the outer ring into chunks, then cut the remaining cake into wedges.

Black Forest Trifle

Cinde Shields
Issaquah, WA

Trifle is a beautiful sight to behold, with its many luscious layers peeking out through an elegant glass bowl. I love preparing trifle because it is so quick & easy and it works with whatever flavors of cake, pie filling and pudding you have on hand!

3.4-oz. pkg. cook & serve
   chocolate pudding mix
8 to 9-inch chocolate cake or 12
   chocolate cupcakes, cut into
   bite-size cubes

21-oz. can cherry pie filling
12-oz. container frozen whipped
   topping, thawed

Prepare pudding mix as package directs; chill in refrigerator. Crumble a few cake pieces; set aside. In a large glass trifle or serving bowl, layer half the remaining cake cubes, followed by pie filling, chocolate pudding and remaining cake cubes. Top with whipped topping. Sprinkle with reserved cake crumbs. Refrigerate until serving. Serves 10.

For a perfectly smooth finish when you're frosting a cake with buttercream frosting, dip a metal spatula in very hot water, wipe it dry and gently glide the spatula over the frosting.

Sweet Treats to
Share

White Chocolate Mousse Trifle

Karen Perkins
Maynardville, TN

This is always the first dessert to disappear at my family gatherings!

18-1/2 oz. pkg. German
    chocolate cake mix
3-oz. pkg. instant white
    chocolate pudding mix
3-oz. pkg. instant chocolate
    pudding mix

4 c. milk, divided
16-oz. container frozen whipped
    topping, thawed and divided

Prepare cake mix according to package directions; bake in a
13"x9" baking pan. Cool completely. Cut into 2-inch cubes; set aside.
Prepare each pudding mix separately according to package directions,
using 2 cups milk for each. Refrigerate puddings for one hour. Stir half
the whipped topping into each pudding. Arrange 1/4 of cake cubes in
a trifle bowl. Spread half of chocolate pudding mixture over cubes.
Arrange 1/4 of cubes over chocolate pudding and top with half of white
chocolate pudding mixture. Repeat layers, ending with white chocolate
pudding mixture. Refrigerate until ready to serve. Serves 10 to 12.

White Chocolate Pie

Beverly Morris
Norman, IN

*I have to prepare this pie every Christmas for my husband...he can't
make it through the holidays without it!*

2 3-oz. pkgs. instant white
    chocolate pudding mix
1-3/4 c. milk
8-oz. pkg. cream cheese,
    softened

12-oz. container frozen whipped
    topping, thawed
9-inch graham cracker crust

In a bowl, combine dry pudding mix and milk. Add cream cheese; beat
with an electric mixer on medium speed until smooth. Gently fold in
whipped topping; mix well. Spoon pudding mixture into crust;
refrigerate for 2 hours before serving. Serves 8.

Kringler

Gloria Morris
British Columbia, Canada

*My son-in-law makes this dessert every Christmas. It is
so yummy and a real treat!*

2 c. all-purpose flour, divided
1/2 c. chilled butter
2 T. ice water
1 c. water
1/2 c. plus 1 T. butter, softened
   and divided

3 eggs
1 t. almond extract, divided
1 c. powdered sugar
2 to 3 T. milk
Garnish: sliced almonds

In a bowl, blend one cup flour, chilled butter and ice water with a
pastry blender until mixture is crumbly. Stir with a fork until a soft
dough forms. Divide dough in half. On 2 parchment paper-lined baking
sheets, press dough into 12-inch by 3-inch rectangles, about 1/2-inch
thick. In a saucepan over medium-high heat, bring water and 1/2 cup
butter to a boil. Remove from heat; immediately stir in remaining flour
until smooth. Add eggs, one at a time, beating after each addition.
Stir in 1/2 teaspoon extract. Spoon half of mixture over each dough
rectangle, spreading to within 3/4 inch of edges. Bake at 350 degrees
for 50 minutes to one hour, until golden and puffy. Immediately
remove from baking sheets; cool. Kringlers will shrink and fall. In a
small bowl, mix powdered sugar, milk and remaining butter and
extract. Spread over cooled Kringlers. Sprinkle with almonds. Slice
before serving. Serves 16 to 20.

Empty vanilla bean pods can be used to make vanilla sugar...so
tasty sprinkled over baked goods or fresh fruit. To make some,
simply bury the bean pods in a jar of sugar for a couple of weeks.

Sweet Treats to
🌿 Share 🌿

Toffee Sauce Pudding

Eleanor Dionne
Beverly, MA

*This is just one of my many favorite pudding recipes. We cook
a lot of puddings during the winter!*

1-1/2 c. all-purpose flour
2 t. baking powder
1 t. salt
1/2 c. butter, divided
2/3 c. sugar

1 c. milk
1/2 c. raisins
zest and juice of 1 lemon
1/2 c. light molasses
1-1/4 c. water

In a small bowl, combine flour, baking powder and salt. In a separate
large bowl, beat 1/4 cup butter with sugar until fluffy. Add milk
alternately with flour mixture, beating until smooth after each addition.
Stir in raisins and lemon zest. Spoon into a well-greased 9"x9" baking
pan. In a saucepan over medium-high heat, combine lemon juice,
remaining butter, molasses and water. Bring mixture to a boil. Remove
from heat; pour gently and evenly over batter in pan. Do not stir. Bake
at 350 degrees for 45 to 50 minutes. To serve, spoon into dessert
dishes and drizzle with sauce from the bottom of the pan. Serves 8.

The salt content in salted butter can vary, so it's best
to use unsalted butter when baking and use the precise
amount of salt specified by the recipe.

Candy Cane Chocolate Mousse

Teree Lay
Sonora, CA

I love serving this dessert in individual Christmas mugs...you could use ramekins or custard cups too. The crushed candy canes make it extra-festive!

1 c. dark chocolate chips
1/4 c. milk
1 T. butter
1/2 t. peppermint extract
3/4 c. pasteurized egg whites
   or 6 pasteurized egg whites

1/8 t. salt
2 T. sugar
Garnish: peppermint candy
   canes, crushed

In a double boiler, melt chocolate chips with milk and butter; stir until smooth. Remove from heat; stir in peppermint extract. Meanwhile, beat egg whites and salt with an electric mixer on high speed until soft peaks form. Add sugar; beat until stiff peaks form. Remove one cup of egg white mixture and stir until smooth. Stir smooth egg white mixture into chocolate mixture until well blended. Fold in remaining egg white mixture with a spatula until no white streaks remain. Divide among 8 custard cups; freeze for 20 to 25 minutes. At serving time, sprinkle each cup with crushed candy canes. Serves 8.

To easily crush candy canes for holiday garnishes, place
candy in a plastic zipping bag and tap gently with
a wooden mallet or rolling pin.

Sweet Treats to
❧ Share ☙

Peppermint Ice Cream Truffles

*Stefanie Schmidt
Las Vegas, NV*

Many of my friends love the seasonal flavors of ice cream available only during the holidays, so I created these truffles for an extra-special treat!

1 pt. peppermint ice cream
3 1-oz. sqs. semi-sweet baking
   chocolate

Garnish: peppermint candy
   canes, crushed

Line a baking pan with parchment paper. Using a melon baller or small ice cream scoop, scoop out 12 small balls of ice cream. Insert a toothpick into each ball; place in pan and transfer to freezer. In a double boiler, melt chocolate slowly. Dip frozen ice cream balls into melted chocolate; quickly roll in crushed candy canes. Remove toothpicks. Transfer to a chilled serving bowl and serve immediately, or freeze in an airtight container. Makes one dozen.

Kids' Favorite Chocolate Sauce

*Nancy Reese
Venice, FL*

This is absolutely one of our family's favorite recipes for the holidays! It is so easy to make...and it's especially fabulous over peppermint ice cream.

1/2 c. butter
12-oz. pkg. semi-sweet
   chocolate chips

1/3 c. evaporated milk
Optional: 1 c. chopped nuts

In a double boiler over medium heat, melt butter, chocolate chips and milk. Stir until chocolate is melted. Remove from heat; stir in nuts, if using. Serve over ice cream; sauce will harden into a shell. Store any leftovers in a tightly sealed glass jar in the refrigerator. Reheat in a pan of water. Serves 6.

Swedish Custard Pudding

Karen Minser
Marshalltown, IA

This recipe is in honor of Mayne Darnell, who was a major in the Salvation Army. She brought this dish to every church supper. She was a wonderful minister...she fed our spirits as well as our bodies.

6 eggs
4 c. milk
1 c. sugar
1/8 t. salt

2 c. quick-cooking rice, cooked
1/2 t. cinnamon
1/8 t. nutmeg

In a large bowl with an electric mixer on medium speed, beat eggs until light and fluffy. Add milk; beat 2 to 3 minutes. Add sugar, salt, rice and cinnamon; mix well. Pour into a lightly greased 8"x8" baking pan. Sprinkle with nutmeg. Bake, uncovered, at 350 degrees for 30 minutes, or until a knife tip inserted into the center comes out clean. Serves 8 to 10.

Make fragrant fire starters from ingredients found around the kitchen. Mix together one-inch cinnamon sticks, dried orange peel and whole cloves. Tuck inside a cardboard tube and wrap the roll with kraft paper, securing the ends with twine. Toss several in a tote for a unique gift.

Index

Index

Index

Have a taste for more?

We created our official Circle of Friends so we could
fill everyone in on the latest scoop at once.
Visit us online to join in the fun and discover free
recipes, exclusive giveaways and much more!

www.gooseberrypatch.com

Call us toll-free at 1·800·854·6673

U.S. to Canadian recipe equivalents

Volume Measurements

1/4 teaspoon	1 mL
1/2 teaspoon	2 mL
1 teaspoon	5 mL
1 tablespoon = 3 teaspoons	15 mL
2 tablespoons = 1 fluid ounce	30 mL
1/4 cup	60 mL
1/3 cup	75 mL
1/2 cup = 4 fluid ounces	125 mL
1 cup = 8 fluid ounces	250 mL
2 cups = 1 pint =16 fluid ounces	500 mL
4 cups = 1 quart	1 L

Weights

1 ounce	30 g
4 ounces	120 g
8 ounces	225 g
16 ounces = 1 pound	450 g

Oven Temperatures

300° F	150° C
325° F	160° C
350° F	180° C
375° F	190° C
400° F	200° C
450° F	230° C

Baking Pan Sizes

Square

8x8x2 inches	2 L = 20x20x5 cm
9x9x2 inches	2.5 L = 23x23x5 cm

Rectangular

13x9x2 inches	3.5 L = 33x23x5 cm

Loaf

9x5x3 inches	2 L = 23x13x7 cm

Round

8x1-1/2 inches	1.2 L = 20x4 cm
9x1-1/2 inches	1.5 L = 23x4 cm